ASTON VILLA'S **PREMIER LEAGUE**

Sport Media
A Trinity Mirror Business

ABOUT THE AUTHOR

Rob Bishop has followed the fortunes of Aston Villa since March 1987 – just before they were relegated to the old Second Division.

Since those dark days, he has been fortunate enough to cover their promotion back to the top flight, two League Cup triumphs, an FA Cup final, numerous ventures into Europe – and more than 500 Premier League matches.

Rob began his career as a junior reporter at the *Dudley Herald* in 1968 and subsequently worked as a sports sub editor on the *Express & Star* before covering non-League football and other local sport for the *Sandwell Evening Mail*.

He then moved to the company's head office, covering Villa, other Midland clubs and England internationals for both the *Birmingham Mail* and the *Sports Argus* before joining the *Birmingham Post* as football correspondent after Euro '96.

In 2001, he joined Villa's new in-house media department as senior writer for the club's various publications, including the award-winning match programme the *Villa News & Record*, the *Claret & Blue* magazine and the *Aston Villa Yearbook*.

He lives with his wife Norma in Wombourne, Staffordshire, and has two married daughters, Louise and Helen, plus a grandson, Taylor.

Sport Media
A Trinity Mirror Business

Published in Great Britain in 2007 by:
Trinity Mirror Sport Media,
PO Box 48, Old Hall Street,
Liverpool L69 3EB

Executive Editor: KEN ROGERS
Art Editor: RICK COOKE
Editorial Assistant: JAMES CLEARY
Cover Design: GLEN HIND

ISBN 978-1905-26628-9

Printed and finished by Brolink

ACKNOWLEDGEMENTS

Overleaf you will find a list of the people who helped in my quest to establish Aston Villa's Perfect 10 Premier League players. I would like to thank all of them for their input, even if we can't claim to have arrived at a definitive list. Once the votes had been cast and the calculations had been made, I thought it would be interesting to see how many of us named all of the players featured in these pages. The answer was none of us – which proves that football really is a game of opinion.

While I'm grateful to every member of the judging panel, two, in particular, have given me invaluable assistance. Journalist Richard Whitehead of *The Times* and statistician Frank Holt, who both have an encyclopaedic knowledge of Villa, kindly offered to act as my editors, checking manuscripts to ensure that everything is factually correct. I couldn't have wished for better-informed or more enthusiastic support.

I am also indebted to another lifelong Villa fan, John Gould, who has compiled books of newspaper cuttings on Villa since the early 1950s, and donated his impressive collection to the club in 2004. John's books, together with various editions of the *Aston Villa Review*, have provided an essential source of reference.

CONTENTS
Perfect
10

	PAGES
The Panel	6-7
Foreword by Martin O'Neill	8-9
Introduction	10-19
Paul McGrath	20-39
Dwight Yorke	40-59
Mark Bosnich	60-81
Dean Saunders	82-101
Andy Townsend	102-119
PICTURE SECTION	120-137
Ian Taylor	138-155
Gareth Southgate	156-175
Paul Merson	176-195
Dion Dublin	196-215
Gareth Barry	216-233
Aston Villa in the Premier League	234-249

THE PANEL

More than 80 people offered their opinion on Villa's Perfect 10 Premiership players, ranging from former players and managers to journalists and supporters. Here is the panel of judges, in alphabetical order.

Charlie Aitken
Brett Ashcroft
Ron Atkinson
Dominic Bant
Gary Birch
Andy Blair
Rob Bishop
Ian Bourne
Paul Brackwell
Dave Bridgewater
Pam Bridgewater
Mark Brooks
Paul Brown
Andy Burrows
Hannah Burrows
Stephen Busst
Ronnie Byrne
Jeff Calvert
Paul Calvert
Nick Clitheroe
Geoff Coleman
Karl Court
Gordon Cowans
Anne Edwards
Allan Evans
Clive Evans
Mark Field
James Gorton
John Gould
Malcolm Greatrex

John Greenfield
John Gregory
Andrea Hartman
Richard Heath
Pat Heard
Graham Hill
Bill Howell
Frank Holt
Dave Ismay
Barry Jackson
Bryan Jones
Phil Lees
Brian Little
Clive Lyons
Tony McAndrew
Alan McInally
Stephen McGrath
Brian Marshall
Phil Mepham
Dan Meredith
Adrian Milledge
Alan Miller
Vic Millward
Bob Moore
Neil Moxley
Paul Murall
Tim Nash
Anne-Marie Newey
Michael Bundgaard Nielsen
David Platt

Jeffrey Prest
Duncan Riddle
Neil Rioch
Derek Russell
Janine Self
Gary Shaw
Craig Simmonds
Janet Simpson
Barrie Smith
Lisa Smith
Steve Stride
Martin Swain
Graham Taylor

Alan Thomason
Craig Trouth
Dave Tysoe
Jim Walker
Jack Watts
Rob Watts
Richard Whitehead
Adrian Williams
Neville Williams
Dave Woodhall
Helen Woolridge
John Wragg

FOREWORD

It was July 1980. Nottingham Forest had won a second successive European Cup two months earlier and we were back in pre-season training with a pronounced spring in our step.

I felt bold enough to ask the great man himself, Brian Clough, who had been his favourite-ever player. Di Stefano, maybe? Puskas? Perhaps even the wonderfully gifted Raich Carter of Middlesbrough and England?

"Yes son, all great players," he replied. "But I would choose myself because I believed that supporters came to see me perform."

I should have expected nothing less from him, but I genuinely believe there's much in Brian Clough's answer when great players take a quiet moment to reflect on their ability.

They might not wish to express their view quite as forcefully as Brian did, but nevertheless that self-belief and touch of arrogance are definitely in the make-up of all great players. Which leads us to this book.

Fans have always had a special place in their hearts for magnificent footballers, be it a goalkeeper who thwarts attack after attack, a resolute and courageous defender, a creative genius in midfield, an exciting winger or a great goalscorer.

Aston Villa have had all of these in their midst over the course of their incredible history. Yet would every member of the 1897 double-winning team have made the list of Villa's greatest players, even if this book had been written as long ago as 1907?

Selecting a club's best players is always going to be difficult, even in this case, where the choice had been narrowed down to recent times – the Premiership years, to be precise.

That means it obviously precludes famous names like Charlie

Athersmith, Joe Bache, Billy Walker, Harry Hampton, Pongo Waring, Eric Houghton, Johnny Dixon, Peter McParland and many of the wonderful League Championship and European Cup-winning team of the early 1980s. Those great players and many others should rest easily, knowing they have not been overlooked. It's just that this book concentrates on Villa's modern era.

I asked Rob Bishop one question only. Was he looking for someone who has been outstanding for Aston Villa for a substantial period, or perhaps someone like David Ginola, a superb player who graced White Hart Lane with his sublime talents but who wore the Villa shirt with a little less distinction?

The answer from Rob was loud and clear. He wanted to focus on players who had made an impact for Villa in the Premier League – and he enlisted the help of supporters as well as former managers and players to get as close as possible to a Villa Premier League Perfect 10.

Anyway, I was delighted to be asked to write a foreword. I was equally delighted at not being asked to make the choices!

Martin O'Neill

Perfect 10 candidates Steve Staunton and Ray Houghton (above, in action against former club Liverpool), and Mark Bosnich (below)

Here are the votes from the Danish judges...

It wasn't quite like the Eurovision Song Contest, but there were times when it felt like it.

Establishing Villa's Perfect 10 Premiership players was no easy matter, which is why I enlisted the help of supporters around the globe, including Michael Bundgaard Nielsen in Denmark.

I also asked people who have watched the team week in, week out over the 15 years of the Premier League's existence, as well as members of the club's backroom and administrative staff, plus former players and managers.

When I undertook this project I was told the choice was entirely mine, if I wished. But partly in the cause of democracy – and partly because I didn't want people accusing me of being way off-beam with my selection – I sought a cross-section of opinion. The results indicated that it was the correct decision, because votes were cast for no fewer than 30 of the 129 players who have represented the club since the formation of the Premier League in 1992.

Some players received no more than a solitary vote – obviously cast because they were personal favourites, for whatever reason. Others seemed to be in contention as the initial votes rolled in but then faded and barely had a mention later on. One or two came up on the rails in the home straight.

To give an example of how diverse the voting was, Ugo

Ehiogu and Kevin Richardson were among the chasing pack by the latter stages of the race, yet both had been early front runners – and Ehiogu was actually top of the list submitted by our Danish judge.

It was fascinating to watch a pattern emerge as more and more people offered their views and gradually it came down to a case of 10 from 12 as a considerable gap developed between the top dozen and the rest of the field.

To be more precise, it was a question of three cast-iron certainties, and then seven from nine. And if there was a gap between the top 12 and the rest, the leading trio were way out in front. There wasn't single person who didn't vote for Dwight Yorke, while Paul McGrath and Gareth Barry were both just one short of a "full house." In Barry's case, I suspect he was merely overlooked by mistake, although McGrath's missing vote was more calculated.

I expressed surprise when club photographer Neville Williams didn't include Macca in his Top 10 but the explanation was logical enough, given that Neville has to produce pictures for Villa's various publications. "I never really saw McGrath," he said. "My lens is always focused on the other end of the pitch!"

Allowing for the two anomalies regarding McGrath and Barry, it's fair to say the top three were unanimous choices and that they would head the chart if a similar poll were conducted on match day at Villa Park.

All right, so Yorke may not have left in the best of circumstances when he headed off to Manchester United in 1998. But the affection he commanded during nine years at Villa Park is undeniable – and with the passing of time, people prefer to remember what he did while he was with the club rather than the unfortunate manner of his departure. No player has scored more goals for Villa in the Premiership but it wasn't merely his prolific output which made him so popular. He played with a smile on his face, he was flamboyant, he was cheeky. As my daughter said when he left for Old Trafford: "They won't love him like we did, will they?" You know, despite a treble triumph in his first season with United, I don't believe they did.

Similarly, McGrath, who played for Villa and United in reverse order to Yorke, was always regarded more fondly in claret and blue than he was in red, even though he helped United to FA Cup glory in 1985.

Nearly a decade later he was back at Wembley in a Villa shirt, helping the club to a League Cup triumph over United in 1994, followed by another against Leeds United two years later. Long before those successes, though, he had come to be regarded as a god because of his majestic performances at the heart of the defence.

If Yorke is the most lethal striker of the Villa's Premiership years, and McGrath the most stylish defender, Barry is undoubtedly the most versatile player of all. Essentially a midfielder of considerable influence, he initially made his name as a central defender – and won his first half-dozen England caps at left-back. While that is far from his favourite position, he can perform there with poise and confidence whenever the need arises. Ask Villa supporters to name their current favourite, and the vast majority will come up with GB.

With three names automatically on the team-sheet, the next task was to eliminate two from the other nine on the short list. It was very nearly Mission Impossible. As the voting fluctuated, certain names dropped out of the top 10 and then back in again. Eventually, the axe fell on Olof Mellberg and Steve Staunton and I can already hear justifiable yells of protest on behalf of both.

Many people would argue, in fact, that the Swedish centre-back has been the club's most consistent performer since his arrival from Spanish club Racing Santander in the summer of 2001. His debut in a goalless draw against Tottenham Hotspur at White Hart Lane on the opening day of that season ranks alongside the best of any Villa new-boy and he has subsequently displayed calm authority in virtually every game in which he has played.

His strong tackling and sense of anticipation have made him one of the most reliable defenders in the country and if his form dipped slightly during the 2005-06 campaign, that can be attributed to injury problems and a difference of opinion with manager David O'Leary.

In general terms, he is the epitome of composure. Like his countryman and former five-times Wimbledon champion Bjorn Borg, he is very much the Ice Man. You get the impression he would have been equally successful if he had pursued his intended career path in tennis, rather than switching to football.

As it was, he went on to become captain of both his club and his country, although he has missed out here to Gareth Southgate, who did likewise for Villa and England. While the intention of this book isn't to establish an actual line-up of Villa's leading Premiership stars, it was certainly a close call between these two. Magnificent as Mellberg has been, Southgate was equally commanding. He possibly got the nod because he was a member of the hugely successful 1995-96 team and also led out Villa for the last FA Cup final to be staged at the old Wembley Stadium.

Staunton, meanwhile, was a magnificent performer over the course of two spells spanning a dozen years. Initially signed from Liverpool by Ron Atkinson in 1991, he returned to Anfield in the summer of 1998 but was brought back to Villa Park by John Gregory two-and-a-half years later.

An intelligent footballer and a great competitor with a left foot to die for, he was a member of the 1994 League Cup-winning side, although he had to settle for a seat on the bench at Wembley two years later, when his season was punctuated by injury and fierce competition for places. He made a total of 350 appearances for Villa, and only 18 players have played more games than that in the club's history. One of them is Barry, who reached 352 at the end of the 2006-07 season – and who was fast-tracked to the first team partly because of Staunton's departure in 1998.

But Mellberg and Staunton are not the only players with every right to feel aggrieved at not making the Perfect 10. As I mentioned earlier, there was also solid support for Kevin Richardson and Ugo Ehiogu before they drifted out of the reckoning.

Richardson, signed from Spanish club Real Sociedad in 1991, was the driving force of Villa's midfield over the next three seasons, missing only two league matches out of 126 during that period, both of them through injury. He was also the captain, and was voted Man of the Match when Ron Atkinson's side outwitted Manchester United at Wembley. The hard-working Geordie had already won league championship medals with Everton and Arsenal but his delight as he paraded the cup in front of the massed ranks of Villa supporters was undisputable. Not long afterwards he was back at Wembley to win his first England cap in a 5-0 thrashing of Greece. He was never selected again, but no Villa supporter would have denied him the right to say he had represented his country.

Ehiogu was an unknown when he was snapped up for just £40,000 from neighbours West Bromwich Albion a month before Richardson's arrival. Despite a promising start, he endured a performance which could easily have wrecked his career in the early part of the inaugural Premier League season. Every pass he made seemed to find a yellow shirt in a 3-2 home defeat by Norwich City, and he was even ridiculed by a piece of graffiti on the dressing room wall at the club's Bodymoor Heath training ground. It read: 'Ugo Ehiogu – Norwich City player of the year, 1992-93'!

But his strength of character is underlined by the way he recovered from that nightmare display by going on to become a permanent fixture at the heart of Villa's defence, as well as being picked for England on a couple of occasions.

He is also one of a select band of 34 players to have made more than 300 league and cup appearances for the club, and his former defensive partner Paul McGrath has no hesitation in naming him in his Villa Dream Team. "He was such a strong human being," says Macca. "He intuitively knew the positions I would take up."

Alan Wright is another player with justifiable cause of complaint at not featuring in the Perfect 10. Like Staunton, McGrath, Ehiogu and Gareth Barry, he, too, is a member of Villa's 300 Club and he was a consummate professional throughout his eight years with the club.

Signed from Blackburn Rovers in March 1995, he quickly established himself as Villa's regular left-back, and the fact that he stands only 5ft 4ins was never an issue. Despite his lack of height, he won his fair share of heading duels and always went about his business, both on and off the pitch, with a quiet dedication that was a trademark of his career.

He was Villa's Mr. Dependable for much of the 1990s, a reliable defender with wonderfully quick feet. And while he scored only five times during his lengthy spell with the club, each of his goals was a spectacular long-range shot.

If Wright received rather less support than I had expected, it was also something of a surprise that the only other player to receive more than the odd vote was Savo Milosevic. While numerous others made themselves unpopular because of the manner in which they left the club, it's fair to say that the Serbian striker was actually despised by most Villa fans after spitting in their direction during a humiliating 5-0 defeat at Blackburn Rovers in January 1998.

It was a stupid act by a frustrated footballer, yet several members of the voting panel felt he was worthy of a chapter in this book. As it is, he will have to settle for a paragraph praising the deft touch of his left foot, his superb dipping shot for the opening goal in the 1996 League Cup final, and his decisive strikes in the home legs of UEFA Cup-ties against Bordeaux and Steaua Bucharest. Had he stayed, I'm convinced he could have become one of the most prolific marksmen of the club's modern era. Instead, his departure was inevitable after he cleared his throat and aimed at visiting fans on Ewood Park's Darwen End.

To offer a brief flavour of the players who also received a mention or two, no fewer than five goalkeepers figured in the voting process. Nigel Spink, one of the heroes of the 1982 European Cup triumph, was the man between the posts at the dawn of the Premiership, while David James, Peter Schmeichel and Thomas Sorensen have recently occupied the custodian's role with distinction. Schmeichel, in fact, is the only keeper to score a competitive goal for Villa and when he fired home at Everton in October 2001, just a month short of his 38th birthday, he also became the club's oldest-ever goalscorer!

But the weight of opinion was firmly with Mark Bosnich, the Australian who was in goal for the largest chunk of Villa's Premiership existence. Controversial he may have been, but Bozzie was an exceptional keeper who helped the club to two League Cup triumphs.

Defensively, Shaun Teale was the only other player to feature in the poll, and it's difficult to argue against a rugged, uncompromising centre-back who never let the side down and was a tower of strength alongside McGrath in the '94 Wembley victory over United.

In sharp contrast, there was a host of midfield candidates, with votes cast for Ray Houghton, Lee Hendrie, Tony Daley, George Boateng, David Ginola and Gavin McCann, while four strikers attracted moderate attention.

Dalian Atkinson, Darius Vassell, Luc Nilis and Juan Pablo Angel are the quartet in question. Belgian marksman Nilis clearly received a sympathy vote after suffering a career-ending double fracture of his right leg in only his third Premiership game, although it was a little surprising that the other three didn't generate more backing.

Ultimately, though, the three "automatic choices" – Barry, McGrath and Yorke – were joined by a goalkeeper, Bosnich, a central defender, Southgate, plus three midfielders and two strikers.

Two of the middle men were 30 by the time they arrived at Villa Park and neither came cheaply, Andy Townsend costing £2.1m from Chelsea in 1993 and Paul Merson £6.75m from Middlesbrough five years later. Yet they weren't looking for an easy ride in the twilight of their careers, both giving four seasons of excellent service.

Townsend, desperate to win a major trophy after losing five semi-finals with three different clubs, was granted his wish in his first season in claret and blue as his powerhouse displays helped to secure the League Cup – and he was back at Wembley two years later, this time as a proud captain lifting the same trophy.

Merson, on the other hand, was a Wembley loser in the 2000 FA Cup final but his magical displays enchanted the Villa faithful. Despite various off-the-field problems, he was a joy to watch as he sprayed inch-perfect passes to all areas of the pitch.

Ian Taylor was equally popular, for totally different reasons. Unlike Merson, he would never claim to have been a flair player but when it came to sheer graft, he had no peers. His work-rate as a "box-to-box" midfielder was phenomenal and his commitment to the club unquestionable. Not really surprising, that. He had been a Holte Ender as a boy.

Like Townsend and Merson, striker Dion Dublin was also something of a "golden oldie" when he was lured across the Midlands from Coventry City in a £5.75m deal in November 1998. Once again, a considerable outlay for a comparatively old head (he was five months short of his 30th birthday) proved to be fully justified.

An amazing start yielded seven goals from his first three games and while he was never likely to maintain that sort of explosive form, he was a constant threat to opposition defences as well as being an inspirational figure in the Villa dressing room. He was brave, too. How many other players would have battled back from a broken neck to score the winning goal in an FA Cup semi-final just three-and-half months later?

The line-up is completed by another prolific goalscorer. Dean Saunders was Villa's first major signing of the Premiership era when he arrived from Liverpool for a club record £2.3m in September 1992, and once again it was money well spent.

He was on target twice in his home debut – a 4-2 victory over his former Anfield colleagues – and went on to score a total of 49 in 144 games over the course of three seasons before joining Turkish club Galatasaray.

That's our Perfect 10, then, although eagle-eyed Villa supporters will no doubt have noticed there is no mention here of a certain Gordon Sidney Cowans. The reason is simple enough. Although Sid ranks as one of the club's all-time greats, he only played 11 Premiership games and six cup-ties for Villa in a fleeting third spell in claret and blue between June 1993 and February 1994. His other 512 appearances for the club had all been made in the days when the top flight of English football was known as the First Division.

In any event, a single chapter would hardly have done justice to a Villa legend who returned to the club yet again, this time in a coaching capacity, after the curtain had fallen on his glorious playing career. I'm just proud that he agreed to serve on the expanded "jury" who helped me reach a verdict on Villa's Premier 10.

Rob Bishop

1989-1996

Paul
McGrath

He had a real stinker that day. Highfield Road was shrouded in mist, but it was nothing compared to the fog in Paul McGrath's head. He didn't have a clue what he was doing, and it showed. At one stage in the first half, he ventured forward for a Villa corner and was still in the goalmouth long after Coventry City had cleared the danger, aimlessly looking around him and obviously uncertain about what to do next.

Even from a distance, the glazed look said it all. An excess of festive cheer had taken its toll, and McGrath, for once, was hopelessly unable to cope. Sky Blues striker Micky Quinn, hardly the most athletic of footballers, scored twice and created the other goal in a 3-0 Boxing Day home win.

And Mr. McGrath? He was more like Mr. Magoo, the blundering, near-sighted children's cartoon character. He has since admitted that he was in no fit state to be playing any sort of football, let alone a Premier League Midlands derby.

But why, you may ask, highlight a dreadful performance by a player who served Villa so well and was revered as a god among the Claret and Blue faithful?

The answer is simple. This was such a rare event that it stands out vividly in the memory, while hundreds of other games have long since been forgotten. Like England's World Cup captain Bobby Moore and Germany's majestic Franz Beckenbauer, McGrath elevated the normally negative business of defending to an art form, to the point where you almost took his superlative displays for granted.

It was only when he (very occasionally) slipped below his own impeccable standards that you really took notice. By his own admission, the Republic of Ireland international took his celebrations a step too far that Christmas. Most supporters were aware he had a drink problem but never before had it been evident in a competitive Villa match. Previously, with the exception of a pre-season friendly in Dublin, where he had fallen over while taking a free-kick, he had always managed to recover by kick-off time. Maybe he would have done so on Boxing Day 1992, had the game started at 3.00pm rather than at noon. We will never know the answer to that one.

What we do know is that two days later, he faced a much more difficult opponent in Ian Wright, and barely allowed the Arsenal striker a kick as Villa beat the Gunners 1-0. If the Claret and Blue faithful had been seething over the previous match, Macca earned their forgiveness in the best possible manner.

Then again, he probably knew he would be able to win them round. That was never more evident than when he went AWOL before a third round FA Cup tie at Exeter in January 1994.

"One of the loveliest memories I have," he says, "is how the fans reacted after I - how shall I put this? - 'went missing' on one occasion.

"I was concerned they would hammer me but at the next home match there was a sign on the Holte End with a Guinness emblem and the words 'Paul McGrath, Pure Genius'. Not only had they forgiven me, they were actually singing my praises. I still have a photo of that. It was one of the most touching moments of my life."

He sometimes drove his managers – even the easy-going Ron Atkinson – to distraction. But Macca could do no wrong in the eyes of those who admired him from the terraces. Some purchased replica shirts bearing the No 5 and the word God;

others bestowed upon him the title Paul McGrath MoM. Certainly, he must have lost count of the times he was voted Man of the Match.

And all the time he was battling to overcome alcoholism. His drink problems are well documented in his powerful autobiography *Back from the Brink* and I don't intend to rake over them all again here, although I once had an insight into just how dependent on booze he had become.

As the Villa reporter for the *Birmingham Mail*, I accompanied the team on a pre-season trip to Hanover in 1991, staying in the city centre while Big Ron and his squad were based at a countryside retreat 18 miles away. The manager was aware I had a hire car, so he asked if I would drive to the airport to pick up Paul Mortimer, a midfielder he had signed from Charlton Athletic just before heading to Germany. Then, to return the favour, he allowed me to travel on the team coach to a friendly in a village near Bremen later the same day.

It was nearly midnight by the time we returned to Villa's hotel but a few of the players were clearly in the mood for a late-night drink. As the coach eased on to the hotel car park, Gordon Cowans sat down beside me and asked: "If you're going back to Hanover, would you mind taking four of us with you?"

I wasn't at all sure this was a good idea, either for me or the players, and particularly not if Ron happened to find out. But Gordon, one of the nicest and most unassuming blokes you could meet, was in persuasive mood. Sensing my unease with his request, he reminded me that the boss had earlier indicated the players were welcome to indulge in a drink or two as a reward for some excellent pre-season preparations.

All the same, I don't think Atkinson had envisaged any of his squad actually leaving their hotel and something told me the players concerned were likely to be found out. The quartet – Cowans, McGrath, Kevin Gage and striker Gary Penrice – had asked me to wait a while so they could change from their tracksuits into something more suitable for the nightlife of Hanover. So it must have looked suspicious when, having refused Ron's offer of a room for the night, I was still hanging around the hotel reception area 20 minutes later.

"You still here?" asked assistant-manager Jim Barron as he emerged from the corridor leading to the bedrooms, to which I spluttered something about trying to translate the following day's lunch menu.

Given that I could neither speak a word of German, nor was I going to be around to sample the restaurant's delights 12 hours later, this was a pretty lame excuse, but Jim merely nodded and told me to drive carefully. Almost as soon as he had disappeared down the corridor, the 'Gang of Four' appeared in the foyer and said they were ready to go.

At this stage, I wasn't unduly concerned about the consequences of providing a lift into the city for a quartet of footballers. Why should I worry? All I had to do was to provide the transport and pack myself off to bed. I should have known better. We were barely clear of the hotel driveway when my passengers asked if we could stop briefly at a bar in a tiny village a mile down the road. As we walked through the door, it was evident this wasn't the first time my pals had popped in for an illicit drink. They were greeted like long lost friends by three or four of the locals.

Apart from a swift half litre of lager, the purpose of this early hours visit turned out to be advice on where to find somewhere lively in Hanover at 1.00am. Armed with information about a disco which would be open for several hours yet, we set off again, my partners-in-crime relaxing after their 'loosener' in the village local.

Once in Hanover, we located the establishment which had been recommended and fought our way to the bar, where Gordon ordered five lagers. I was barely a third of the way down mine when, amid the throbbing noise of the music, Paul asked in his appealing Irish lilt: "Another one, Rob?"

I tried to yell back that the one in my hand would do me nicely, thanks, but it was too late. Having picked up a full glass from the bar, Paul passed it to me with a smile. "I got you one in," he smiled, his own second glass having already been relieved of a generous gulp or two.

Paul McGrath's boozing binges are legendary, but this was the first time I'd been involved in one – or, at least, witnessed the early stages of one.

Half-an-hour or so later I headed back to my hotel, so quite how things developed in the early hours, or how the Villa lads got back to their own hotel 18 miles away, I never did discover. In any event, it was none of my business. Or so I thought. The next morning, I made a routine call to Ron Atkinson to check if there was any news for that day's edition of the Mail.

"No, I don't think so," he said. "But one question before you go - which four did you take into Hanover last night? I know McGrath and Cowans went with you. Who were the others?"

How on earth did I get out of this one? The last thing I wanted was to land the players in trouble, but Ron clearly knew something untoward had happened and I didn't want to sour my relationship with him just a couple of months after his appointment. As the Mail's Villa man, I was likely to need the new manager's co-operation for the foreseeable future. I tried stalling.

"They're not in trouble, are they?" I spluttered.

"No," he replied, "but they'll know about it in training this morning!"

If Atkinson made light of that situation, he wasn't quite so sympathetic when McGrath repeated the heavy booze session on a couple of other occasions during that trip, once climbing out of his bedroom window and slipping down a drainpipe to get to the bar. By the start of the season Ron was ready to offload his problem and, having already sold striker Tony

Cascarino to Celtic, there seemed every possibility that the Parkhead club might also relieve Villa of their talented but mentally scarred defender.

It was a move, McGrath has since revealed, that would have suited him down to the ground, but the deal fell through and Atkinson was subsequently happy to acknowledge he had a lucky escape. Maybe Villa would have enjoyed similar success over the next three seasons anyway, even without McGrath at the heart of their defence, but I wouldn't advise suggesting the notion to anyone who watched Villa regularly around that time.

In Atkinson's first season at the helm, the team finished eighth in the First Division and reached the quarter-finals of the FA Cup, McGrath forging a solid central partnership alongside Shaun Teale, a rugged, uncompromising player who had been recruited from Bournemouth and who more than lived up to the manager's prediction that while he wouldn't sell many season tickets, he would make life tough for opposing strikers.

A year later, Villa were runners-up to Manchester United in the inaugural Premier League campaign – and McGrath was acclaimed PFA Player of the Year, having also won his club's award for the fourth consecutive season as well as being voted the Midlands' top player. But the PFA award was clearly the one which gave him most satisfaction. It is the highest accolade any footballer can receive and he has described the occasion as "the proudest day of my life."

The following March, he helped Villa to a 3-1 Wembley victory over Manchester United in the Coca-Cola Cup final, despite having been up all the previous night in agony with a frozen shoulder and having required three or four pain-killing injections before the match and another one at half-time.

McGrath may have been in agony before kick-off but he was magnificent that day. Although he could barely lift his arm, he shackled United's main danger man Mark Hughes until the 83rd minute, when Hughes scored following a corner. By then, though, Villa were two-up through Dalian Atkinson and Dean Saunders, who rounded off a memorable victory with a late penalty.

There's little doubt that mental strength, as much as his natural talent and physical power, saw him through that glorious afternoon at Wembley, when Villa supporters out-sang and out-chanted their red and white counterparts from an hour before kick-off until long after the final whistle had blown.

United went on to win the Premiership title and the FA Cup, so Villa denied them a domestic treble that season, and victory was particularly sweet for the man who had been shown the door by the Old Trafford club five years earlier.

Alex Ferguson had made it clear from day one in the United hot seat that he was unwilling to tolerate the booze culture which revolved around McGrath and his two drinking partners, Bryan Robson and Norman Whiteside. There was an air of inevitability in the summer of 1989 when Whiteside was transferred to Everton and McGrath made the move which would be the making of his career.

It didn't quite seem that way initially, of course. United had attempted to cut their losses on the troubled Irishman by trying to persuade him to retire on the basis of his dodgy knees and walk away with an insurance pay-out of £100,000.

"I was asked to quit football and make myself a lot of money from the insurance," he said at the time. "But I think I still have a lot to offer football. It's my life. I would rather they kept the money than give up football."

Within a few weeks of moving to Villa Park, he was probably having second thoughts on the subject – and his new manager was certainly wishing McGrath had taken the money and run.

Graham Taylor had decided to take a £425,000 gamble on McGrath's defensive experience in the wake of a difficult campaign in which Villa had only narrowly escaped a quick return to the old Second Division following their elevation to the top flight 12 months earlier.

Taylor unquestionably needed cover at the back. Martin Keown had moved to Everton earlier in the summer, while the veteran Allan Evans, despite having played a major role in Villa's First Division survival, was approaching his 33rd birthday and didn't figure in the manager's long-term plans. To plug the gaps, Taylor snapped up Kent Nielsen from Danish club Brondby and then made his move for McGrath - but not before consulting Ron Atkinson, who had been McGrath's boss at Old Trafford when United won the FA Cup in 1985.

Ironically 'Big Ron', by then manager of Sheffield Wednesday, had also spoken to Ferguson about taking McGrath off his hands, but was only willing to offer an initial £150,000. He knew, however, that Villa could meet United's asking price, and gave Taylor an honest assessment of someone he considered to be a wonderful player and a lovely guy.

By October, though, it was all going horribly wrong. Wonderful player or not, McGrath was such a tormented soul that he attempted to slash his wrists, an action which was more a cry for help than a genuine serious suicide attempt. Yet the episode remained a closely-guarded secret, even when he returned to action wearing wristbands three weeks later!

The cover-up was helped, in part, by the fact that at the time he attacked himself with a Stanley knife in desperation he was actually injured anyway, having pulled a hamstring in a League Cup tie against Wolves.

During his absence, Villa reeled off three consecutive league victories, Nielsen forming a solid central defensive partnership with Derek Mountfield, so when McGrath returned to the fold in the home match against Everton early in November, he was handed a midfield role, with the specific task of marking his old pal Whiteside.

He did the job so successfully that Villa ran out 6-2 winners, although he was rather less effective in subsequent defeats by

West Ham and Norwich City before putting in another good display in a 4-1 home win over Coventry City.

Then came the radical move which shaped the remainder of the season. Wimbledon had been Villa's bogey team since gaining promotion to the top flight, winning three and drawing one of four league encounters between the sides as well as delivering a fourth round FA Cup blow the previous season.

Coming to terms with the Crazy Gang's unconventional, uncompromising style would continue to be a problem for Villa for some years to come, but at Plough Lane on the last Saturday of November, Graham Taylor's decision to revert to a 3-5-2 formation completely baffled the upstarts from south London.

David Platt and Tony Daley were the scorers in a 2-0 win but the foundations for victory lay in a formidable three-man back line of Mountfield, Nielsen and McGrath, whose outstanding performance completely disguised his off-the-pitch problems and convinced a relieved Taylor that the £425,000 had, after all, been money well spent.

From that juncture, Villa were never outside the top three and for a four-month period they were constantly in the top two, eventually finishing runners-up to Liverpool.

They even reached the summit after a magnificent 2-0 midweek success at Tottenham in February, only to inexplicably slump 3-0 at home to Wimbledon the following Saturday, a match in which many supporters believe the title slipped away. A win that afternoon would have taken Villa five points clear but the setback had a devastating effect on their confidence and they scored only eight goals in the next 11 games.

If there was one constant during the course of an inconsistent run-in, it was the form of Paul McGrath. He even scored his first goal for the club in a 3-3 home draw against Norwich on the penultimate weekend, and deservedly shared the Midland Soccer Writers' Player of the Year award with Platt, who also scooped the PFA award. As Taylor later reflected: "I was Paul's club manager for only one season, but it was one to remember. And I reckon the money we paid for him was a shrewd piece of business for Aston Villa."

From a purely personal point of view, the most satisfying result for McGrath that season was undoubtedly a 3-0 Boxing Day home victory over United as Villa's title bid clicked into overdrive.

Yet it was during the build-up to that game that I had my first insight into his fragile temperament. The *Birmingham Mail* wanted an in-depth interview ahead of McGrath's first match against the Reds since being booted out of Old Trafford, and he agreed to meet me at Villa's Bodymoor Heath training ground. But it was one of the most difficult interviews I have ever conducted.

Some footballers have little to say; others can occasionally be unhelpful just for the sake of it. In Macca's case, there was clearly a lot more going on in his mind than Aston Villa v Manchester United, even though that was the only subject on the agenda.

We hadn't really spoken to each other before, so his caution was understandable to a point, but each time I asked a question his eyes narrowed with suspicion before he carefully delivered his answer.

But if time eases pain, it also breaks down barriers. Within 18 months, as I have already related, we were enjoying a beer together in a German nightclub and while that didn't exactly make us bosom pals, it at least showed he had come to trust me.

And just imagine how flattered I was when, four years later, I was asked to produce a brochure for his testimonial match at Villa Park. The request didn't come directly from Macca, he was much too shy for that, but from Frank Mullen, who had been his manager at Irish junior club Dalkey United.

Frank was very much a father figure to Paul so it was fitting that he should be chairman of the committee which organised a 'double' testimonial, comprising a friendly match against Villa's deadliest rivals Birmingham City at Villa Park and a dinner in Dublin a few weeks later.

Gathering material for the brochure proved to be one of the easiest tasks I've ever undertaken. Every journalist I approached, both national and local, was only too happy to wax lyrical about the man who had given them so much pleasure.

Glancing through that brochure all these years later, it's tempting to suggest that the nine reporters who composed tributes were competing with each other to come up with the most impressive one-liner to describe Macca's extraordinary talents.

Andy Colquhoun of the *Birmingham Post* talked about his "sublime, unhurried football"; the *News of the World's* David Harrison claimed his courage and pain threshold defied all medical logic; Martin Swain of the *Express & Star* described him as a "constant and crazy contradiction." Perhaps the most apt description of all, though, came from the man from the *Daily Express*.

"Give him understanding and a gentle discipline," wrote John Wragg, "and he will repay you with champagne football."

There was no problem, either, in getting people in the game to sing Macca's praises. His former Villa managers Taylor and Atkinson both delivered glowing tributes, as did his current boss Brian Little and Republic of Ireland manager Jack Charlton.

Villa team-mates Dean Saunders, Steve Staunton and Andy Townsend offered their thoughts, too, Townsend describing his Republic colleague as a Rolls Royce of a footballer.

"He just comes out at weekends," said the midfielder. "He fires first time, cruises for 90 minutes and is then put away again. Yes, he's that good, and both Villa and Ireland are fortunate to have such a prestigious model on the car park."

Then there was physio Jim Walker, the man who did more

than anyone to ensure McGrath was in the best possible condition whenever he pulled on a claret and blue shirt.

Walker didn't merely tend to the Irishman's knees (more often than not while the rest of the squad were training); he also acted as a nursemaid throughout all his troubles. He was the perfect man for the job, a gentle soul who was always willing to sit and listen, and McGrath has described him as "my vital support system."

For his part, Walker never questioned why the bravest of footballers could act almost like a child when he wasn't on the pitch. He merely appreciated an exceptionally gifted individual, suggesting that Paul was unique among modern-day footballers – "he gives the impression he would still be as majestic as ever if he went on the pitch wearing a collar and tie!"

The testimonial game attracted just over 12,000, which was a disappointing turnout for such a revered player. In fairness, though, Villa fans had more important things on their minds that week.

A depressing early-season sequence, which had yielded a solitary point from nine Premiership games, had resulted in Atkinson being sacked after a 4-3 defeat by Wimbledon at Selhurst Park in November. His successor, Brian Little had initially turned things around, but the threat of relegation still loomed large on the night of McGrath's match. Villa needed a point from their visit to Norwich the following Saturday (an objective they duly achieved) so perhaps supporters were not in the mood for a friendly against Blues, even for the benefit of Mr. McGrath.

The 1994-95 season had been a real shocker for Villa, even though McGrath had performed consistently, appearing in all but three of the team's 52 league and cup matches. His importance was never better illustrated than when he was relegated by Little to the subs bench for the Boxing Day clash against Arsenal at Highbury.

Villa seemed destined for defeat when Andy Townsend was sent off with more than half-an-hour to play but 20 minutes from time Macca replaced Dean Saunders and the score remained goalless. Afterwards, a frustrated Gunners manager George Graham told the Villa boss he knew it would finish 0-0 once McGrath had gone on.

If the proceeds of his testimonial game were considerably less than we had anticipated, Paul had no hesitation in displaying his gratitude for my efforts on his behalf.

Any journalist who sits on a footballer's testimonial committee undertakes the task on a voluntary basis and a simple 'thank-you' is the only payment required. But my reward for producing Paul's brochure was an invitation for my wife Norma and I to spend a weekend in Dublin a month later and attend his Irish testimonial dinner at the plush Burlington Hotel.

It was an unforgettable experience. Apart from sampling the delights of Dublin's fair city, we also attended the Republic's World Cup qualifier against Austria at Lansdowne Road and then found ourselves seated at the top table at the dinner, along with the Ireland squad, manager Jack Charlton and singer Frances Black, who had taken a break from her UK tour to sing a couple of songs. That's how highly Paul McGrath is regarded across the Irish Sea.

The function was also attended by Villa chairman Doug Ellis, who delivered a moving speech in which he referred to Paul as "my son," and the defender had no problems with that.

"Doug always looked after me and put an arm around my shoulder when I had any problems," he says. "Whenever I was coming towards the end of a contract I used to panic, fearing I wouldn't be offered a new one, but he always took me to one side and assured me everything would be sorted out."

If the 1994-95 campaign was one to forget, the following season was a huge success, for Villa in general and McGrath in particular. He turned 36 that winter but his performances were as commanding as ever and his team-mates reaped the benefits. With Ugo Ehiogu and new arrival Gareth Southgate equally impressive alongside him, Villa conceded just 35 league goals, the same number as champions Manchester United and a figure bettered by only Liverpool and Arsenal.

With the addition of summer signings Southgate, midfielder Mark Draper and striker Savo Milosevic, Villa finished fourth in the league and reached the semi-finals of the FA Cup. But their crowning glory was an emphatic 3-0 Wembley triumph over Leeds United as McGrath collected his second League Cup winners' medal in the space of three seasons.

In the dressing room afterwards, while most of his team-mates celebrated in boisterous fashion, he sat quietly in one corner, no doubt reflecting on the success which had come his way in a claret and blue shirt.

He will forever be grateful to Graham Taylor for signing him, no question about that. And his popularity with supporters has, if anything, grown even stronger down the years.

When he visited Birmingham to promote his autobiography, he was besieged by autograph hunters and well-wishers at Villa's city centre store, and when he made an appearance at half-time in the following day's match against Fulham, he was given the same tumultuous ovation which had been afforded to new manager Martin O'Neill a few weeks earlier.

"I was overwhelmed by the reception," he admits. "I couldn't quite believe how the fans were. Then again, I couldn't really comprehend it when I was playing, either. When you're a footballer, people tend to elevate you to a status that you find hard to believe. I could never envisage myself living up to that hero worship. We are all flawed. It used to amaze me the way the fans were. I wanted to do well for them because of the way they treated me.

"Villa Park is the place where I played the best football of my career. I couldn't have imagined that when I left United. It was supposed to be downhill all the way after you left Old Trafford but there were some great people at Villa and they couldn't have been more helpful. I will always be grateful to Villa for extending my career and enabling me to play alongside some great players."

Sadly, all good things come to an end, and despite Villa's success in 1995-96, the signs were there that McGrath's days in claret and blue were numbered. Little had become the first Villa manager to drop the seemingly evergreen Republic of Ireland international, relegating him to the bench on four occasions and although the player was handed a new one-year contract that summer, his time on the pitch amounted to around half-an-hour.

An unused substitute in the opening nine matches, he was finally called into action for the final 29 minutes, plus stoppage time, of the second leg UEFA Cup tie away to Helsingborgs of Sweden. Ironically, it was a substitution laced with attacking intention, McGrath taking over from Portuguese full-back Fernando Nelson so that Ugo Ehiogu could push forward in search of the goal Villa desperately needed to reach the second round.

It didn't materialise, Villa went out on the away goals rule and McGrath wasn't even on the bench when they lost the next Premiership match, 4-3 at Newcastle. By the time they slipped to a 1-0 defeat at Tottenham 12 days later, a magnificent Villa career was over. McGrath had joined Derby County.

It would be unfair, even with the benefit of hindsight, to criticise Little for selling arguably the best-loved player in Villa's history. By then, Gareth Southgate and Ugo Ehiogu had established themselves as the regular central defensive pairing in a 4-4-2 formation, and the team enjoyed another successful campaign, qualifying for Europe once again with a finishing position of fifth.

But by way of a gentle reminder that it might have been better still, McGrath reserved two of his best Derby performances for Villa's visits to the Baseball Ground.

Villa supporters gave their departed hero a warm reception both before and after a fourth round FA Cup tie in January, but in between times he offered no courtesy to his former colleagues, inspiring the Rams to a 3-1 victory. And he was even better in the league match between the sides in April, nullifying the threat of Dwight Yorke and Savo Milosevic as Derby won 2-1 on the day Villa goalkeeper Mark Bosnich stormed out of the ground an hour before kick-off after being told he wasn't in the starting line-up.

McGrath also won 51 of his 83 Republic of Ireland caps while he was a Villa player, switching effortlessly from his defensive position in claret and blue to the midfield role he occupied for the national side. His more advanced position resulted in him scoring eight international goals, only one less than he managed in 323 appearances for Villa.

He twice represented his country at World Cup finals, in Italy in 1990 and the USA four years later, although his countryman and former club colleague Steve Staunton believes his definitive display in the green shirt of Ireland was in the 1-1 draw against England at Wembley in 1991.

"Paul's really outstanding displays were as a commanding defender," says Staunton. "But I rate that performance against England as the best of his career. There's no doubt in my mind that Paul was the cornerstone of the Irish team, first of all running the show as a midfielder and later providing a tower of strength of the heart of the defence.

"His level of performance was so high that a bad game for him would have been an average one for most other players. And at his best, he was absolutely magnificent."

It's been said, in fact, that McGrath is his country's most loved sportsman, even if he also happened to be the least understood. National affection for him was perfectly illustrated when Nelson Mandela's first visit to Ireland coincided with the arrival at Dublin airport of Jack Charlton's team.

Understandably, there was quite a gathering to welcome both the anti-apartheid hero and the footballers, and when Mandela's was the first recognisable face to appear, there was a loud chant of "Ooh, aah, Paul McGrath's dah!" That was a fair indication of the esteem in which Macca is held in the country which has been his homeland since his mother took him there as a baby.

He may have driven his various managers to distraction with his off-the-field problems but there's no denying the fact that McGrath was the complete footballer. During his time with Villa, he played alongside Kent Nielsen, Derek Mountfield, Shaun Teale, Ugo Ehiogu and Gareth Southgate. All of them were quality centre-backs in their own right, yet they all benefited from having the great man as a partner. So did Kevin Moran before them at Manchester United.

"Paul McGrath is the best centre-half I ever had in any of my teams," says Ron Atkinson, his manager at both Old Trafford and Villa Park. "He would be an automatic choice in my team of all-time greats."

Dwight Yorke, another player who helped to illuminate the Atkinson era at Villa, agrees. "Paul was arguably the best player I ever played with and the best player in the world on his day," says the man from the Caribbean. "If I could describe him in one word it would be 'phenomenal.' Strikers must have felt it was impossible to get past him."

And how about this glowing tribute from Charlie Aitken, Villa's record appearance holder?

"Paul is without doubt the best centre-half I have ever seen at Villa Park. He was world class, no question about it. He was simply brilliant. I haven't seen a better reader of the game – no-one else comes near him in that respect. He was phenomenal and Villa supporters quite rightly regarded him as a god."

Journalist Tom Humphries, meanwhile, knows all about the depth of feeling for Macca across the Irish Sea.

In a poignant and compelling article about Macca's struggles with alcoholism, Humphries wrote: "He is aware of the warm place he has in the national bosom. People would pay higher taxes if it meant seeing him well and happy and better."

Villa supporters might just have an issue with the business of paying higher taxes but they would happily cough up a small fortune for the privilege of watching McGrath display his uncanny anticipation or make one of his unconventional back-heeled clearances, which initially seemed to border on reckless but were ultimately accepted as part of McGrath's make-up. As a TV commentator once remarked, it was as if they had given him the script beforehand.

There's perhaps just one question we haven't asked, but one lifelong Villa supporter, clearly a Doctor Who fan, comes as close as humanly possible to providing the answer.

"Until someone invents a real Tardis, time travel seems unlikely," says Richard Whitehead. "So we will never know if McGrath was the best Villa player of all time or whether that accolade belongs to Billy Walker. Who cares? What is surely indisputable is that McGrath is the club's finest post-war player."

Not many Villa folk will disagree with that sentiment, even if we all too often took Macca's genius for granted. Then again, it was staring us in the face for more than seven years.

PAUL McGRATH - CAREER STATS

BORN:	Ealing, London
DATE OF BIRTH:	December 4 1959
JOINED VILLA:	August 1989
VILLA LEAGUE APPS:	253
GOALS:	8
VILLA CUP APPS:	70
GOALS	1
INT. CAPS (Rep. of Ireland):	83
GOALS:	1

1989-1998

Dwight Yorke

"I bet you £100 that my bag comes through before yours."

Dwight Yorke was in mischievous mood, but Mark Bosnich didn't want to know. "No way," he replied. "You're always taking money off me."

We were standing in the arrivals hall at Birmingham International Airport, waiting for the carousel to rouse from its slumbers into the snake-like movement which would deliver our luggage. It was 2.00am and everyone was feeling pretty weary following the flight home from France, where Villa had forced a goalless draw against Bordeaux in the UEFA Cup.

Effervescent soul that he is, though, Yorkie was in the mood for a wager. And as there was no football, horse racing or flies climbing up walls to entice him, the Trinidad & Tobago striker had turned his attention to the stationary carousel.

But Bosnich was in no mood to risk losing a hundred quid, even with a 50-50 chance of success. The Australian goalkeeper had suffered too many losses to his team-mate in the past to risk another one.

He once made the mistake, for instance, of accepting a bet that his pal couldn't keep a football in the air with his head 100 times while standing in the restrictive confines of a doorway at Villa's Bodymoor Heath training ground.

As Dwight effortlessly passed the century mark while chatting to those who had gathered to witness the event, he offered

Bozzie the chance of double or quits. Goalkeepers may have a reputation for being mad, but the Aussie custodian sensibly decided to cut his losses.

At Birmingham Airport in September 1997, though, Bosnich missed a glorious opportunity to redress the balance. His case didn't merely put in an appearance ahead of Yorke's luggage, it was actually the first to show when the conveyer belt finally got moving. He grabbed it angrily before heading off into the night, cursing his inability to get one over his team-mate.

As Bozzie disappeared from sight, I asked Dwight if he had really intended betting £100 on his case against Bozzie's. "Of course," he replied. "Do you want the bet now he's gone?" I declined. "Not me, mate," I told him. "I don't earn the sort of money that you get."

From beneath his back-to-front baseball cap, he beamed a typical white-toothed grin. "I probably don't get as much as you think," he replied. "But I'm very happy!"

Nine months later, Yorke was far from happy. For eight-and-and-half years he had been feted as a hero at Villa Park; now his head had been turned by interest from Manchester United. Alex Ferguson wanted him, and suddenly, understandably, he was wondering what heights he might scale with one of the top clubs in the world.

The summer of 1998 was a distressing time for Villa. Big name players Savo Milosevic and Steve Staunton both left, Stan Collymore was in trouble for assaulting his girlfriend Ulrika Jonsson in a Paris bar, David Unsworth signed from West Ham and then declared he had made an almighty mistake because he should really have joined Everton, where he eventually ended up without ever kicking a ball in competitive action for Villa. As manager John Gregory later put it, he seemed to spend all his time "putting out fires."

Yorke's fire, unfortunately, just kept on burning. Having maintained a diplomatic silence for most of the close season, he finally declared that yes, he really would like to leave Villa and join United, prompting the widely-publicised quote from Gregory: "If I'd had a gun right then, I would have shot him."

It was perhaps as well that Gregory didn't have a weapon to hand, and not just for the sake of Yorke's state of health. When the deal eventually, inevitably came to fruition, it was one which was beneficial all round.

Apart from collecting a cool £12m from the biggest sale in their history, Villa rarely noticed the departure of their star player, going a dozen games unbeaten – their best-ever start to a league campaign. Yorke, meanwhile, helped United to a league, FA Cup and European Cup treble in his first season at Old Trafford. And the VAT man wasn't complaining at his nice little cut of £600,000.

The nature of Yorke's departure, unfortunately, meant he has never been forgiven by Holte Enders, who have given him a hostile reception on his subsequent visits with United and Blackburn Rovers.

That's a great pity, because rarely have Villa folk taken a player so much to their hearts. They watched him arrive from Tobago as a wide-eyed 17-year-old, highly ambitious but far from sure of himself in a foreign land, and evolve into one of most gifted players ever to pull on the famous claret and blue shirt.

Yet he might never have made it to these shores if Villa hadn't endured such a torrid time during the 1988-89 campaign. Promoted back to the top flight the previous season, they were, by March, facing the grim prospect of going straight back down again.

That's why manager Graham Taylor took them off to the Caribbean to recharge their batteries during an extended break in the league programme. Apart from relaxing in the sun, the team also played a couple of friendly games, one against the Trinidad & Tobago national side, the other against a Tobago XI. Yorke was involved in both, and at half-time in the second match, which had kicked off an hour late because of scorching temperatures, Taylor asked if he would like to switch to the Villa team, just to see how he would cope alongside professional players.

Watching Yorke in action sent a tingle down the manager's spine, which is why the bright-eyed teenager and 20-year-old Colvin Hutchinson were offered trials with Villa early the following season.

It was hardly a major 'scoop' but I took a certain amount of pride in breaking the story in the *Birmingham Mail*, in a five-paragraph story headlined: 'Villa put Trinidad teenagers on trial.' The headline wasn't exactly accurate, given the fact that Hutchinson had turned 20 in June, but it was clear from Taylor's quotes which player he regarded more highly.

"They came to our attention when we played a Tobago XI on our trip to the West Indies in March," he told me. "Yorke really took the eye, although he was still at school then, so we invited them over."

During the course of the next few weeks, Yorke made such an impression that he was offered a contract worth £120,000 – small fry by today's inflated football salaries but more than he had ever dreamed about. It was a fair return on the £80 outlay he had splashed out on the silver-grey suit – together with a handkerchief in the top pocket – in which he had arrived for his trial. And it wasn't long before he started to make his presence felt.

Of course, Yorke offered far more than what he perceived to be the typically English way of dressing. He may have been slight and slender, sometimes with the look of a little boy lost, but give him a football and he was a flamboyant showman, conjuring up all manner of tricks. That ball-juggling feat in the doorway was typical of his incredible skills, and Taylor recalls another occasion when he walked all the way from the training pitch to the Bodymoor Heath dressing room – around 200 yards

– with a ball balanced on his head.

He immediately displayed his predatory instincts, too, scoring four times in a friendly at Telford, and after some outstanding performances for the reserves he was given a taste of first-team action when he replaced Tony Daley for the final eight minutes of a 1-0 defeat at Crystal Palace at the end of March, followed by a 14-minute run-out at home to Manchester City a week later.

That was the sum total of his involvement as Villa finished runners-up to Liverpool in 1989-90, but his potential was immense. Just ask Taylor, who headed off that summer to accept the role of England coach.

"My biggest regret in leaving Villa was Dwight," said the manager. "I knew I was leaving behind someone who was going to be a world-class player."

Another ex-Villa boss most certainly didn't share that opinion. The following season, with former Czech coach Dr. Jozef Venglos at the helm, Yorke was in the starting line-up on 11 occasions and also scored a couple of goals. But Tommy Docherty, who had managed Villa in the late sixties and early seventies, was far from impressed with the youngster's full debut against Manchester United on the last Saturday of December.

At the time, Docherty wrote a regular column for the *Sunday Mercury* and a week after the 1-1 draw at Old Trafford, 'The Doc's Casebook' delivered a damning verdict on the debut boy's performance.

"If that lad makes a First Division footballer," he wrote, "my name is Mao Tse-tung. He looks frightened every time he touches the ball. His first instinct is to pass back instead of having the confidence to beat his defender."

They were harsh words, indeed – and comments which might have destroyed a more fragile character. But there was never any question about Yorke's mental strength. He just needed toughening up a bit, and Ron Atkinson set about that particular task after replacing Venglos the following summer. One of Atkinson's first signings was Ugo Ehiogu from neighbours West Bromwich Albion, and the powerful central defender was under orders to put in some hard challenges on his slightly-built team-mate, who many people considered too frail for the physical nature of English football.

Even Dwight admitted to having a few reservations, particularly when Ron Atkinson recruited experienced strikers Cyrille Regis and Dalian Atkinson shortly after taking over as manager. The youngster was deeply concerned that those signings would see him slip down the pecking order with little prospect of regular first-team football.

As it happened, I was able to reassure him that he was very much a part of the manager's plans, having put the question to Ron during a pre-season trip to Germany and received an answer which I knew to be genuine. The manager insisted he had great faith in the young striker and it cheered up Dwight no end when I told him what his boss had said.

Ron was as good as his word. Yorke was in the line-up for the first two games of the season and it wasn't long before his beaming smile was signaling some fabulous goals – none better than his breathtaking individual effort against Nottingham Forest just a few weeks into the new campaign.

Receiving the ball from Kevin Richardson deep in his own half, he sprinted to the edge of the Forest penalty area, left defender Brett Williams on his backside with a clever turn and floated the ball tantalisingly over goalkeeper Mark Crossley's outstretched fingertips.

It was a goal laced with power, pace, poise and precision, and was almost as good as the spectacular solo effort produced by Dalian Atkinson against Wimbledon just over 12 months later.

In the following Monday's *Birmingham Evening Mail*, I described Yorke as a "lithe and lively athlete whose potential is higher than the proposed new Witton Lane Stand." I also called him the Calypso Kid, a nickname which understandably stuck as he continued to weave his Caribbean magic at Villa Park. It was also one of the few occasions on which he acknowledged something which had been written about him.

A few days after he had mesmerised Forest's defence in a 3-1 victory, Villa played at Grimsby in the League Cup, and the Press facilities at Blundell Park were basic, to say the least. Essentially, there was nowhere to interview players after the game, so I ventured down to the visitors' dressing room in search of a post-match quote or two.

By the time I got there most of Villa's players had left, but as I popped my head around the door, Dwight was sitting on his own in the corner. He didn't have a great deal to say about the goalless draw which had just taken place, but grinned at me and said: "Calypso Kid, eh? No problem!"

Later that season, Yorke achieved another milestone, his first hat-trick in a competitive professional match – and it should really have been four. While he was on target three times in a thrilling 4-3 win at Derby in a fourth round FA Cup tie, he also missed two penalties! Both kicks were saved by former England goalkeeper Peter Shilton, although Yorke at least netted the rebound after his first effort had been pushed out. All four Villa goals – Garry Parker was also on target – came in a 31-minute spell in the first half, which was an incredible scoring burst, given the fact they had managed just one in the previous 564 minutes of action!

Shortly after the Derby game, David Platt, the player Villa had sold to Italian club Bari for £5.5m in 1991, was back in the Midlands to promote a range of shin pads. If anyone could provide an accurate appraisal of his former team-mate, Platt was the man.

"Dwight and I used to stay behind after training when we played together at Villa," he said. "I used to help him, but he was also willing to help himself. We always knew he had great potential but he needed to build up confidence and to be a little more ruthless in terms of what he wanted to achieve. Now it's all starting to pay off. Dwight has the talent to do something special in every game. He's quick, he's nimble on his feet and he has good balance."

And yet Yorke still had a few self-doubts, as I began to appreciate during Villa's 1992 pre-season tour to Berlin and Dresden. While he had come on leaps and bounds in a relatively short space of time, Dwight knew he also had a long way to go. He was basically still a shy, reserved young man when we headed for Germany, still not altogether sure of himself in the company of the team's star players. One evening after dinner, as Dalian Atkinson held court about how he made regular trips to Sheffield to spend a small fortune on designer clothes, Dwight looked in envy and astonishment at the sort of prices his team-mate was willing to pay for a suit. His own salary obviously didn't yet allow such extravagances.

If the launch of the Premier League was viewed as an exciting new era for the game in this country, Yorke didn't quite see it that way - initially, anyway. Having played in 61 games over the course of the two previous seasons, scoring 19 goals in the process, he managed only another 49 appearance during the first two campaigns of the Premier League and scored only a dozen times. He didn't even have the satisfaction of playing in the club's first game in the new league, a 1-1 draw at Ipswich, because he was away with Trinidad & Tobago for a World Cup qualifier.

When he returned, he found it difficult to re-establish himself in the side, particularly after Dean Saunders arrived from Liverpool for £2.3m and forged an effective striking partnership with Atkinson. All the same, Yorke at least enjoyed an extended run after Christmas and, typically, came up with two BBC Goals of the Month, both of them in 2-0 home successes. The first, against Ipswich Town was a diving header from Steve Staunton's left-wing cross following a neat build-up involving Steve Froggatt and Garry Parker; the second, against Sheffield Wednesday, underlined that not all great goals have to be spectacular long-range shots. The game against Wednesday was barely three minutes old when Ron Atkinson's men created an almost hypnotic move which involved everyone except Shaun Teale and goalkeeper Mark Bosnich before Yorke, six yards out, provided the finishing touch to a true masterpiece.

Such was its quality, the goal evoked memories of Liverpool at their best in the seventies and eighties, or Don Revie's Leeds United, and the young striker later revealed how much he had enjoyed operating just behind the front two of Saunders and Regis.

There was further consolation that season, too, in that Yorke at least played a reasonable part in a Championship bid which eventually faltered over the closing weeks as Villa finished 10 points behind champions Manchester United. But that certainly wasn't the case in 1993-94. For most of that campaign he was sidelined by an injury which meant he missed out on both the club's UEFA Cup ties against Slovan Bratislava and Deportivo La Coruna and, more importantly, the League Cup triumph over Manchester United at Wembley.

In truth, there was no reason why Ron Atkinson should have picked Yorke, who was fit by that stage but had been largely restricted to substitute appearances in the weeks leading up to the final, ahead of the regular pairing of Saunders and Dalian Atkinson. For all that, Yorke was bitterly disappointed that he wasn't even on the bench and even considered packing his bags and heading home to Tobago. He admits it was the worst thing to have happened to him throughout his career.

It crossed his mind, though, that by giving up at that juncture, he would have wasted all the hard work he had put in over the course of four-and-a-half years. His manager's words were still ringing in his ears, too. "Make sure, when Villa come back to Wembley," Atkinson told him, "that you are in the team."

Two years later he would do just that, but even in the midst of that disappointing period in his career, he was still capable of special moments. He netted only three goals in 93-94, but they were all significant. One was the winner in a fourth round FA Cup tie at Grimsby, the other two were of more lasting importance. They were the last to be scored in front of the Holte End terracing.

The vast bank, capable of holding more than 19,000 standing spectators, was demolished that summer to make way for the current double-decker, all-seater stand. But not before Yorke had written himself into claret and blue folklore. He cancelled out Robbie Fowler's early goal for Liverpool with a 65th-minute equaliser before netting the winner nine minutes from time in front of a singing, swaying mass of adoring fans.

Ironically, Liverpool were again the opponents for the final home match the following season, and once again Yorke was on target twice at the Holte End – with a few subtle differences. This time the goals came in the first half; this time the fans were seated; this time a 2-0 win was crucial to Villa's Premiership survival, rather than being merely of sentimental value.

It had been a campaign to forget down Witton way. Despite starting with a five-match unbeaten sequence, the team then went nine without a win, a dismal run which culminated in Atkinson's sacking and the subsequent appointment of Brian Little.

Fortunately, Villa survived with a draw at Norwich on the final day, and while Yorke's output was a modest eight goals, he was in the starting line-up for 39 league and cup matches – his highest figure to date. There's no doubt that the experience he gained from that testing campaign paid handsome dividends 12 months later in what ranks as Villa's most successful

Premiership season to date.

True, they didn't quite match the runners-up spot which had been attained three years earlier. But fourth place was a more than respectable finishing position and Brian Little's men also reached the FA Cup semi-finals for the first time since 1960. Then there was the matter of a second League Cup triumph in the space of three seasons. And there's no doubt that Yorke's goalscoring was the catalyst for his team's success. It should have been profitable for me, too, although ultimately it wasn't.

During the build-up to the 1995-96 season, Dwight's agent Tony Stephens invited me along to a friendly at Molineux between Wolves and Arsenal, with a pre-match meal thrown in. Dwight also happened to be there and, during dinner, he poured me a glass of red wine. I cheekily suggested he should give me a glass for every goal he scored during the coming season and he readily agreed.

He was on fire during the next few months, enjoying his most prolific campaign in claret and blue with a total of 25 goals. At a rough average of five glasses per bottle, that impressive record should have earned me half a case of Bordeaux, but I'm still waiting to raise a glass to his achievement. Whenever we meet, his greeting is always the same: "How you doin'? I still owe you that wine, don't I?"

I've long since given up hope of ever seeing it, but who cares? I was intoxicated with the sheer magic he conjured up as he produced a succession of vintage moments in claret and blue - one of them an 89th-minute goal in an emphatic 3-0 victory over Leeds United in the League Cup final. Having been left out two years earlier, he had taken to heart Ron Atkinson's order to make sure he was in the line-up the next time Villa got to Wembley, and scoring at the famous old stadium was a special moment.

Certainly, he was ever-so-slightly under the influence of a drop of champagne during the post-match dressing room celebrations. As the players happily sipped the customary bubbly from the trophy, the mood became increasingly buoyant and no-one was in higher spirits than Dwight, who gave every indication of having gulped rather more than his fair share. I'll never forget the sight of him standing naked in the middle of the room and bursting forth with the song with which Villa supporters had serenaded him both during and after the final:

> *"Start spreading the news,*
> *He's playing today-ay,*
> *I want to be a part of it,*
> *Dwight Yorke, Dwight Yooooorke..."*

He was no Frank Sinatra, that's for sure, but he quickly found some willing backing vocalists as he belted out the re-written words to *New York, New York*. At first he did, anyway. Half-an-hour and six or seven renditions later, the novelty had worn a bit thin and most of his colleagues had left to join their families for a drink. Yorkie, though, was still going strong.

If that was his crowning glory, though, it was by no means the only one. He was voted Footballer of the Year by the Midland Football Writers and his goal haul included 17 in the league – the highest number from a Villa player since David Platt's contribution of 19 five years earlier.

He also converted all five of the penalties Villa were awarded, a unique feat during the club's 15 Premiership years.

That statistic alone must have been sweet music to the ears of a player who had twice failed from the spot in an FA Cup tie at Derby four years earlier, and none of the quintet of spot-kicks was more delicious than the one he scored against Sheffield United, ironically in another fourth round Cup tie.

By comparison with the 4-3 feast we had witnessed at the Baseball Ground in 1992, goals were in short supply at Bramall Lane, despite Villa's unquestionable superiority. With more than

an hour gone, BBC bosses must have started to doubt their wisdom in selecting the tie for live coverage.

But then came the moment which made it all worthwhile. In the 64th minute Villa were awarded a penalty when Serbian striker Savo Milosevic was brought down by Blades goalkeeper Alan Kelly. Everyone in the ground was convinced Yorke was about to blast his spot kick as he strode purposefully forward, but he suddenly paused and gently chipped a looping shot into the centre of the goal and just under the bar as Kelly dived to his left.

It was described in that year's *Aston Villa Review* as "the equivalent of a Yorker by Brian Lara's former Caribbean cricketing mate" and it was, indeed, an exquisite moment.

Other players have, on rare occasions, attempted to emulate the cheeky ploy, usually with the safety net of their team holding a two or three-goal lead. To execute such an audacious penalty with the tightrope fully stretched at 0-0 in a tense cup tie was astonishing, and said everything about Yorke's laid-back temperament.

His happy-go-lucky approach was again evident when Villa travelled to Spain for a UEFA Cup tie a couple of seasons later. Bilbao Airport is situated between two mountain ranges and we had been warned there was likely to be a fair bit of wind as we made our approach, though nothing could have prepared us for the roller-coaster ride we encountered. It was more like being in a glider than a jet as the turbulent conditions forced the plane both up and down and side-to-side. But in a perverse sort of way, Dwight's prophecy of doom managed to calm everyone's nerves. Breaking off from his card game with team-mates at the back of the aircraft, he announced in a high-pitched voice: "We're going to crash! We're all going to die!"

In different circumstances, it might have created panic, but Dwight's proclamation was somehow reassuring. All the time he was saying it, he had a huge grin on his face. After all, this lad was a regular passenger between Britain and the Caribbean and had no doubt experienced far worse conditions.

Back on solid ground at the end of that season, he was again in impish mood. To secure a UEFA Cup place in 1998, Villa needed to beat Arsenal at home in the final game, and then hope Chelsea beat VfB Stuttgart in the European Cup Winners' Cup final the following Wednesday.

Like the rest of the side, Yorke had been inconsistent for more than half the season; like the rest of the side, he flourished after John Gregory had taken over from Brian Little in February. At the time of Gregory's appointment, Villa stood 15th in the table with just eight wins in 27 games. By the end of the season they were seventh, having won seven of their final nine fixtures.

The last of those successes was by a single goal against the Gunners. Gareth Barry made his full debut that day but the more abiding memory is of Yorke making a fool of England goalkeeper David Seaman in the same way he had outfoxed Sheffield United's Alan Kelly in the FA Cup a couple of years earlier.

Fouled in the area by Gilles Grimandi in the 36th minute, Yorke started his long run-up for the resultant penalty like a West Indies fast bowler. Seaman dived left in the hope of stopping the anticipated ferocious drive – while Yorke, displaying all the finesse of Tiger Woods around the green, chipped a dainty little shot just right of centre. As it skipped over the line, even Seaman couldn't help seeing the funny side, grinning from ear to ear in acknowledgement of having been kidded by a true magician.

In hindsight, how fitting it would have been if that had been Dwight's finale in a Villa shirt. Manager Gregory privately shed a tear of joy a few days later when, during the club's end-of-season trip to Majorca, he learned that Chelsea had won the Cup Winners' Cup and, in so doing, had opened the door for Villa to take part in the following season's UEFA Cup competition. But by the end of that summer, Gregory must have been close to tears of rage as the club's most treasured possession was slowly but surely lured away to Old Trafford. Once news of United's interest had been made public, the saga dragged on through May, June and July, and into August. One week it looked like Yorke would be leaving, the next we were given firm assurances he was going nowhere.

Villa were even prepared to make him the highest-paid player in their history, chairman Doug Ellis attempting to get him to commit his long-term future to the club by offering a five-year deal worth £5m, with the promise of a testimonial in 1999 to mark his 10th anniversary at Villa Park. Gregory, meanwhile, went on record as saying that any club wishing to buy Yorke would have to break the British transfer record, the £15m paid by Newcastle United to Blackburn Rovers for Alan Shearer.

"As far as I'm concerned, Dwight is not leaving," said Gregory at the time. "He has two years left on his contract and he is not going anywhere. United may try to buy him, but I'm not interested."

When August arrived and Yorke was still around, the Villa faithful must have been heartened, particularly as he had avoided making any comment, one way or the other, on where he saw his future – although there was just a hint that he was looking towards Manchester.

On the eve of Villa's return to pre-season training, I quoted him on the subject in the *Birmingham Post*. "Unless I am told otherwise," he said, "I expect to start the season as an Aston Villa player. I have to weigh up everything very carefully, but the fact remains that I still have two years left on my contract, so I'm here to play for Villa for that time, if they want me. But, of course, at the end of two years, I would be free to leave the club for nothing under freedom of contract so I'm sure that will be taken into consideration."

It was a statement, formulated in conjunction with his agent

Tony Stephens, which clearly and precisely stated the facts of the situation and made perfect sense. All the same, you couldn't help thinking that the club were gradually being backed into a corner, and that ultimately they would have no option but to part company with their star player.

The bottom line was that Villa could make a fortune by selling then, or risk getting nothing two years down the line – and once Yorke had told Gregory he wanted to join United, his departure was irrevocably set in motion.

By the time Villa lined up for their opening match of the season against Everton at Goodison Park, most people were resigned to him being gone before the transfer deadline the following Thursday, and so it proved. It's just a pity the move didn't happen earlier, because Yorke did himself no favours on Merseyside as Villa, with their backs to the wall for most of the afternoon, battled doggedly for a goalless draw. It was the first of a record-breaking 12-game unbeaten start for Gregory's men but Yorke's contribution was negligible. He didn't really want to be on that pitch; his mind was clearly elsewhere.

Having eulogised over some of his breathtaking performances for the club, I found it almost painful to report his sub-standard showing in the following Monday's Post. I wrote that 'Yorke, quite simply, was a pale shadow of the flamboyant individual who has headed Villa's score chart for the past three seasons. The man who usually plays with a smile on his face had the look on Saturday of someone with all the cares of the world on his shoulders.'

If the manner of his exit left a bitter taste, though, it has surely been softened with the passing of time. Yorke may have been booed on his subsequent returns to Villa Park with United and Blackburn and he hardly helped to heal the wounds by spending a short spell with Villa's fiercest rivals, Birmingham City. But the vast majority of Villa supporters will always have a soft spot for the man who added flair, flamboyance and fun to Villa's performances over the course of 286 first-team appearances.

He was also on target 98 times, which left him just two short of becoming only the 12th player in the club's history to score a century of goals for Villa. He remains, too, the club's highest Premiership marksman with 60 and, by the end of the 2006-07 season, was one of only half-a-dozen players to have netted a Premier League hat-trick for Villa, along with Dean Saunders, Tommy Johnson, Savo Milosevic, Dion Dublin and Luke Moore.

Typically, there is something about Yorke's hat-trick which sets it apart from the rest. All the others were the highlights of comfortable victories; Dwight did it on a night when Villa contrived to lose! Almost unbelievably, he had failed to score in the opening nine games of the 1996-97 season but he found his touch with a treble at St. James' Park, only for Villa to go down 4-3 in a thriller. To make matters worse, he also had another effort disallowed for offside, a decision which television evidence later proved to be incorrect.

Despite his faltering start to the campaign, he finished with 20 league and cup goals, a figure which put him among the Premiership's top-six scorers, and signed a contract designed to keep him at Villa Park until the Millennium. Little could we have known at the time that it simply wasn't going to happen, and what a pity it didn't. There wouldn't have been a mere testimonial to commemorate his 10 years at the club, more a Caribbean carnival.

DWIGHT YORKE - CAREER STATS

BORN:	Canaan, Tobago
DATE OF BIRTH:	November 3 1971
JOINED VILLA:	December 1989
VILLA LEAGUE APPS:	231
GOALS:	73
VILLA CUP APPS:	56
GOALS	25
INT. CAPS (Trinidad & Tobago):	59
GOALS:	26

1992-1999

Mark
Bosnich

It was just before 2pm as I strolled towards the main gate at Derby County's Baseball Ground in the early April sunshine. All the people around me were total strangers but I was suddenly aware of a familiar figure striding purposefully in the opposite direction on the other side of the street. He passed so quickly that there was barely time to register his face. But I would have sworn it was Mark Bosnich.

Surely not, I thought. Not with barely an hour to go to kick-off. Not unless he was hastily delivering complimentary tickets to someone. No, forget it. It must have been someone who looked like him.

But hey, what was this? Seconds later, dashing through the gate and evidently in even more of a hurry, was Villa's goalkeeping coach Paul Barron, kitted out in shirt, shorts, socks and boots. What on earth was happening here?

In the aftermath of Villa's 2-1 defeat, all was revealed. Bosnich, furious at not being named in the starting line-up, had thrown a tantrum and had walked out of the ground. Barron had desperately been trying to catch up with him to get him to change his mind, but with no success. Adamant he was going nowhere but home, the Australian goalkeeper had hailed a taxi and demanded to be driven back to Birmingham.

"I've never known anything like this," admitted manager Brian

Little, who was clearly distressed by the unfortunate episode, and it was easy to sympathise with the Villa boss. After all, he had merely decided it was too soon for Bosnich to play a full match after recovering from a knee injury. If Little and the rest of the squad were staggered by the goalkeeper's reaction to being named as a substitute, though, perhaps they shouldn't really have been surprised. This wasn't the first time Bosnich had performed a reckless act and it wouldn't be the last. A few years later, he would pay the ultimate price for his controversial nature and hedonistic lifestyle when he was banned for nine months by the FA for failing a drugs test, and subsequently sacked by Chelsea.

Yet he will always have a place in the hearts of Aston Villa supporters who watched him in his prime. The defiant streak, which landed him in so much trouble, also contributed immensely to enhancing his performances between the posts. Maybe his kicking left a lot to be desired (and was at times even subjected to ridicule) but in every other respect he was an exceptional goalkeeper. Confident and commanding, he gathered crosses effortlessly and was an outstanding shot-stopper. And when it came to the toughest task of all, he had few peers. When a team are awarded a penalty, the odds are invariably in favour of the player taking the kick, but that certainly wasn't the case when Bosnich was in goal for Villa. In one unforgettable season, he saved five of the six spot-kicks fired at him – plus another three in one of the most dramatic penalty shoot-outs ever seen.

Call it arrogance, if you like, but Bosnich claimed to have known from the age of 12 that he was destined for greatness. He wanted to be the best keeper in the world, and there was a stage during his time at Villa Park that he wasn't far short of achieving that ambition, only for his suspect temperament to let him down. As much as he craved greatness, he seemed equally determined to self-destruct.

If there was one single moment which encapsulated his career it was surely his incredible save on a February afternoon in 1998. Diving to his right to meet a shot from Coventry City's Trond Soltvedt, he looked beaten as the ball took a deflection off defender Ugo Ehiogu and headed towards the other side of goal. Somehow he managed to switch direction, thrusting upward with his left leg to hook the ball clear. It was an unbelievable piece of athleticism, described in that year's *Aston Villa Review* as "a once-in-a-million save." Yet it counted for nothing as Coventry recorded their first-ever win at Villa Park to reach the fifth round of the FA Cup. Just when Bozzie looked a winner, he ended up a loser.

Nevertheless, he was a charismatic character who proved that football is not just a game for dullards. He was a headline writer's dream, whether he was making saves which were out-of-this world or making a spectacle of himself on and off the pitch. While he commanded thousands of column inches during the course of his career, though, he was – initially, at least – one of the most low-key signings ever made by Villa.

Any journalist will confirm that no matter how much effort you put in, sometimes you stumble across a story by accident. That's what happened to me when Bosnich arrived in the Midlands in February 1992. Villa had just beaten Swindon Town to reach the FA Cup quarter-finals and the *Birmingham Evening Mail* decided that the achievement warranted a special edition of the paper. The day after the 2-1 victory at the County Ground, I was despatched to Villa Park to interview chairman Doug Ellis about his dream of seeing the club at Wembley in the FA Cup Final and he happily reminisced about his visits to the famous old stadium for the club's three League Cup finals of the 1970s.

He was well into his flow when he was suddenly interrupted by a phone call, during which he asked if I would wait in his outer office. I didn't expect him to divulge the nature of the call, but when I returned he told me the club had just completed the signing of a young Australian goalkeeper called Mark Bosnich, who had played three games for Manchester United before work permit problems had resulted in him going back Down Under to play for his hometown club Sydney Croatia.

The permit issue had been resolved because Bosnich was now married to an English girl and had been recommended to Villa by coach Brian Whitehouse, who had known the player during their time together at Old Trafford.

Having given me the details, Ellis even invited me to use his phone to call the office and dictate the story to a copytaker so that it could appear in the day's later editions. It was far from a major story, and the sports editor required no more than a few short paragraphs to record the arrival of a third-choice goalkeeper. By the following morning, the *Birmingham Post* decided that even my brief story was too long, reducing it to a single paragraph at the end of another piece about Villa. Paul McGrath, Steve Staunton and Tony Daley had been forced to withdraw from international duty because of injuries sustained in the Cup-tie at Swindon, and the newspaper, not unreasonably, deemed this information to be of greater interest to their readers.

Their story merely concluded that the club had "insured themselves against a goalkeeping crisis" because Les Sealey faced a four-match suspension after being sent off against Sheffield Wednesday the previous month. "Yesterday", wrote Mike Ward, "(Ron) Atkinson signed 20-year-old Mark Bosnich, the Yugoslav-born Australian international 'keeper, to act as cover for Sealey and Nigel Spink."

The paragraph wasn't strictly accurate. Although his father was Croatian, the player was actually born in Fairfield, Australia. What also went unsaid at the time was that Mark Bosnich's middle name could easily have been 'Controversy'. In fairness, we weren't to know that even his transfer to Villa had been conducted in dubious circumstances until 21 months later, when the club were fined £20,000 and ordered to pay £15,000 costs for breaching rules concerning the signing of players. Although Bosnich had bought out his contract at the Sydney club for £10,000, this was a time when agents were not supposed to receive fees from clubs, and Bozzie's agent, the former West Bromwich Albion goalkeeper Graham Smith, had been paid £150,000 by Villa, plus a further £150,000 for future add-ons. For his part, Smith insisted that everything was above board, suggesting that if it was a question of the interpretation of rules, he was certain there would soon be a change because any number of foreign players moved around the world with the help of agents.

As you might expect, that story generated considerably more space on the back pages than the brief announcement which had greeted the goalkeeper's arrival in the Midlands. By then, though, he was no stranger to headlines, most of them about his superlative performances between the posts.

Yet his introduction to life as a Villa player was fairly low-key, despite complaints from United that he had broken a gentleman's agreement to return to them if ever he were to be granted the work permit they had unsuccessfully sought for him.

Bozzie, though, was adamant he had done nothing wrong. "I had to buy my contract out," he said. "But it was worth it to come back to England. Maybe I could have gone back to United but I didn't exactly turn my back on them. They hadn't really kept in touch – all I got from them was a Christmas card. They did contact me eventually, but by then I had already agreed to join Villa."

Bosnich's debut for Villa's reserves was delayed because international clearance hadn't come through, so he had to wait a couple of weeks before turning out against Sunderland in a 2-2 Pontin's League draw. By the end of the season, he had made a handful of appearances for the reserves, as well as turning out in a friendly against a Bari side including David Platt, who had joined the Italian club the previous summer.

His more significant action, though, was his competitive first-team debut in the penultimate game of the season against relegation-threatened Luton Town at the end of April. Villa lost 2-0 but the goalkeeper's performance was highly encouraging and he certainly couldn't be faulted with either of the Hatters' goals. That afternoon at Kenilworth Road, we were also given the first indication that life with Bozzie would never be boring.

As Luton mounted one of their many attacks, he had to race out of his penalty area and act as a sweeper to halt a run by Mick Harford, forcing the striker into touch. His reaction to a dangerous situation was commendable but he was subsequently booked for holding on to the ball as Luton players attempted to wrestle it from his grasp in order to take a quick throw-in!

Bozzie had to wait more than seven months for his next taste of first-team football, a 2-1 win at Sheffield Wednesday in December, but his big breakthrough came on a night of bitter disappointment for the club. Having just recovered from a shoulder injury, he stepped in for an FA Cup replay against Wimbledon at Selhurst Park after regular keeper Nigel Spink was sent home with a stomach bug. He performed admirably, too, making a series of fine saves in a game which finished goalless after extra-time before Villa were beaten 6-5 in a penalty shoot-out.

Little more than a year later, he would be the hero of another dramatic shoot-out. For the time being, though, the priority was getting established and his display in south London was impressive enough to earn him a regular place for the remainder of the 1992-93 season. Before a 3-0 defeat at Blackburn, in fact, he had kept nine clean sheets in 15 starts and hadn't conceded any more than a single goal in any game.

He also helped to create a piece of English football history when he and Everton's Jason Kearton became the first Australian goalkeepers to face each other in a match in this country, and such was his rapid progress that he was regarded as one of the key figures when Villa headed to Old Trafford in March for one of the crunch matches of the inaugural Premier League title race. The pundits were spot on, too. He was in superb form against his one-time employers, denying Manchester United time and again with some magnificent saves in a 1-1 draw. Who would have believed that 13 months earlier he had seemed destined to become a Sydney beach bum, helping his father build swimming pools and spending his days on the beach?

"His first save from Eric Cantona was tremendous, and the boy made two or three great saves," said United manager Alex Ferguson, who was no doubt more annoyed than ever at Bosnich's decision to revive his English career with Villa rather than the Red Devils. At least Ferguson must have felt he had the last laugh as United went on to become champions, but Bosnich's late-season contribution to Villa's runners-up position was acknowledged as he was deservedly voted the club's Young Player of the Year.

He was a young man with the world at his feet, no question about that, and there was no doubt he would also have started the following season as first choice goalkeeper. But a series of events conspired to ensure that he did absolutely nothing for the first nine matches. During his time back in Sydney, he had become an Australian international, and had represented his country at the 1992 Olympic Games in Barcelona. Now he was required by the Aussies for two World Cup qualifiers against Canada but while he was flattered by the call-up, he turned it down because it coincided with Villa's opening Premiership match against QPR. If he thought it was merely a case of putting club before country, however, he was very much mistaken. FIFA took a dim view of his refusal to play for his country and promptly imposed a worldwide ban on him. If he wouldn't play for Australia, he wasn't going to play against QPR, either.

He eventually made up with his friends Down Under, turning out for the Aussies in the first leg of their World Cup play-off against Argentina in October but it was a frustrating start to the new campaign for him. Villa had a perfectly capable deputy in Spink and the experienced goalkeeper performed so well in the first couple of games that manager Atkinson simply couldn't leave him out.

Who knows, Bosnich may well have been consigned to a place on the bench for the whole of the season but for a situation reminiscent of the club's 1982 European Cup triumph against Bayern Munich. That night in Rotterdam, Spink had performed heroics after taking over from the injured Jimmy Rimmer after just nine minutes; this time, the long-serving keeper was the injured party – and Bozzie came in right on cue to inspire a victory which was more modest, but still provided immense satisfaction to the claret and blue half of Birmingham.

At St. Andrew's on Tuesday 21st September 1993, Bosnich replaced his injured colleague after half-an-hour of a League Cup-tie – and within six minutes he had saved a penalty. Blues midfielder John Frain struck the spot-kick well, but it was at a convenient height for the substitute goalkeeper. "I saw Frain was left-footed and decided to dive to my left," Bosnich explained afterwards. "You could call it a bit of a detective's hunch!"

Hunch or not, he repeated the feat a month later when Villa held Spanish club Deportivo La Coruna to a 1-1 draw in the first leg of a second round UEFA Cup clash, making a save which ranks among the most memorable in the club's history. Just three minutes had elapsed when Deportivo were awarded a penalty and the home crowd were ready to salute the opening goal when their Brazilian striker Bebeto fired his spot-kick

fiercely towards the left-hand corner. It looked a certain conversion but Bosnich reduced the Riazor Stadium to silence as he hurled himself across goal and somehow managed to tip the ball away.

There could have been no better way to start a European debut, and the irony was that Bozzie nearly didn't start the match. At the time, teams were allowed only three non-national players per match and if Irish defender Steve Staunton had been fit, he would have joined his international colleagues Paul McGrath and Andy Townsend in the starting line-up. Rarely can a manager have been so pleased that one of his key players was injured!

Atkinson left no doubt about how highly he regarded Bosnich's penalty acrobatics, describing the save as "unreal" and "the best I have ever seen." Bosnich, for his part, regarded it as the best save he had ever made, and he later gave another insight into a psychological game he had played with the penalty taker. "As Bebeto was placing the ball, he glanced briefly to my left and then took a much longer look to my right," he said. "Then he looked at me. It could have been a double bluff but I made up my mind that I would go left. I feinted to the right first and then took off the other way. Luckily it worked out."

Mark Bosnich had never been short of confidence but it was now literally bursting out of him. As he patched things up with Australia, he declared: "It's always been my ambition to be the best goalkeeper in the world and this is a chance to show my country what I can do."

He was also conscious, though, of not jeopardising his position at Villa, insisting that he delay his flight to Sydney for the game against Diego Maradona's Argentina until after the League Cup-tie against Sunderland at Roker Park. It was as well he did. The record books show that Villa won 4-1 but rarely has there been such a misleading scoreline. The Wearsiders dominated from the outset, and even allowing for Villa's four breakaway goals, Atkinson's men would almost certainly have gone out but for Bosnich's agility. As everyone attempted to come to terms with the incredible contest which had unfolded, Sunderland manager Terry Butcher admitted: "I've not seen much of him before and I don't want to see him again! He's a fabulous keeper with a great temperament. We threw as much pressure as we could at him but he proved he could handle it. He's a hell of a prospect."

The former England defender wasn't alone in his glowing appraisal of Bozzie. Villa's assistant manager Jim Barron, himself an ex-keeper, went even further: "He is the best young goalkeeper in the world, without a shadow of a doubt. And the best thing about Mark is that he knows it. Like all the greats, he is a fanatical perfectionist. At 21, he's already up there with the best shot-stoppers and the cleanest gatherers of crosses in the Premier League. I know all about Aussie cricketers and rugby players but I think Mark can become the most famous Australian sportsman since Herb Elliott."

Bosnich, who missed a 2-1 win at Swindon while he was serving his country, was immediately re-instated for the second leg of the UEFA clash against Deportivo, but was powerless to prevent the first home defeat for one of Atkinson's teams in Europe. His brilliant penalty save in La Coruna was ultimately rendered of only cosmetic value as the Spanish side sneaked away from Villa Park with a 1-0 verdict.

While Villa were out of the hunt for European honours, they were still hot on the domestic trophy trail, taking another stride towards the League Cup final with a fourth-round victory away to Arsenal in late November. Bozzie, though, will more vividly recollect the league meeting between the teams at Highbury three weeks earlier.

In a reverse of the fortunes the two goalkeepers had encountered at St. Andrew's, this time it was Spink's turn to take over between the posts after Bosnich had limped off with a hip injury six minutes after half-time – but not before the Aussie ace had produced another stunning penalty save. In what was almost a carbon copy of his spectacular save in La Coruna, he flung himself to his left to tip Ian Wright's spot-kick on to a post, and once again his team profited immensely. Although Wright eventually put the Gunners ahead seven minutes after Bosnich's departure, the visitors emerged 2-1 winners with late goals from Guy Whittingham and Andy Townsend.

The downside was that Bozzie's injury meant he had to withdraw from the second leg of his country's World Cup play-off match against Argentina in Buenos Aires. Despite round-the-clock treatment from physio Jim Walker, he failed a fitness test, discovering that he couldn't dive on his hip without experiencing considerable pain. As he reluctantly informed Australia of the outcome, Villa came under fire from Aussie coach Eddie Thomson, who suggested the club had put pressure on the keeper not to play for his country. Needless to say, that didn't go down well with Ron Atkinson, who pointed to a club rule which stated a player should pull out of international action if he had failed to complete the previous Villa match.

"The rules apply to everyone, not just the Australians," said the angry Villa boss. "I don't remember Jack Charlton bellyaching when he had to leave Paul McGrath out of a Republic of Ireland international. Mark Bosnich is the same as everyone else. It was obvious he was injured when he came off at Arsenal. The Aussies would also do well to remember that it was us who persuaded Bosnich to play in the World Cup play-offs."

While Australia's dreams of playing in the USA finals the following summer were ended by a 1-0 defeat, their star player continued to be acclaimed by his contemporaries, including two of the best goalkeepers in the Premiership

"Mark is astonishing," declared Manchester United's Peter

Schmeichel. "At the age of 21 he has the confidence of a 30-year-old. He is already on the fringe of world class, and has what it takes to become the best in the world." And Liverpool's Bruce Grobbelaar added: "Mark is the best young prospect I have seen."

Early the following year those views were echoed by pretty much the whole of the football world. When Villa won 2-1 at Tottenham in the fifth round of the League Cup and were then paired with Tranmere Rovers in the semi-finals, everyone was convinced that Big Ron's boys were Wembley-bound. What no-one could have envisaged was that it would take the heroics of a goalkeeper from Down Under to get them there. It looked a hopeless cause, in fact, when Villa trailed 3-0 in the first leg at Prenton Park, but Dalian Atkinson's last-gasp volley offered a glimmer of hope and an 88th-minute header from the same player at Villa Park in the return left the tie deadlocked at 4-4 on aggregate. Extra-time failed to produce a solution to a compelling contest, so it was down to a penalty shoot-out to decide who would be playing in the final. And what drama we witnessed in that shoot-out!

The first five kicks were all converted before Bosnich saved from Ged Brannan to leave Villa ahead at 3-2, but the visitors were back on level terms at 4-4 after Ugo Ehiogu had sent his shot against the bar. The tension was unbearable as Kevin Richardson blasted the next kick high over the bar – the ball striking the window of a North Stand executive box – leaving Liam O'Brien with the chance to give Tranmere victory.

But Bozzie won that particular psychological battle, diving right to smother O'Brien's effort, and after Tony Daley had scored from the first "sudden death" penalty, the Villa keeper leapt to his left to beat away Ian Nolan's shot before bounding in celebration towards the massed ranks of delirious home fans on the Holte End. In the space of a few minutes, he had prevented his side from defeat and then clinched their ticket to

Wembley.

No wonder he and his team-mates were carried shoulder-high from the pitch by jubilant supporters, although the occasion was surrounded by controversy. Far from being a shoot-out hero, Bosnich was depicted as a villain by many observers, who felt he should not have been on the pitch by that stage. There was a strong body of opinion that he should have been sent off for bringing down John Aldridge for the penalty from which the veteran striker netted Tranmere's 29th-minute goal. The Merseysiders even made an official complaint over referee Allan Gunn's decision not to show the red card. Bosnich, being Bosnich, was adamant the ref had got it spot on. "I'm not surprised I didn't get sent off," he said. "I went for the ball fairly and squarely."

He certainly wasn't about to lose any sleep over the incident. Instead, as if to atone for being beaten from the spot by Aldridge, he went to White Hart Lane three days later and saved two more penalties! Darren Anderton fired to Bozzie's right in the 44th minute, Nicky Barmby went left in the 52nd and the outcome was the same on each occasion – another penalty reflex-action save from a young man who had confidence oozing from every pore.

Nigel Spink may have started the season in goal but there was only one man who was going to face Manchester United at Wembley, where Villa outwitted Alex Ferguson's side in a 3-1 victory. Even the displaced Spink couldn't hide his admiration for the 22-year-old, describing him as big, brave and very good at shot-stopping. "He's got all the attributes for the job," said the veteran 'keeper. "His only weakness may be his kicking. The rest is in place. Mark has bags of self-confidence and that's vital to building a career for himself."

If 1993-94 was a glory season for Bosnich and his team-mates, the following campaign couldn't have been more different. It was the season in which Atkinson was sacked and

Villa only avoided relegation on the final day. But while Big Ron was unable to halt the team's slide down the table, he had a few home truths for Bosnich before making his departure.

For instance, after a 3-2 defeat at Anfield, the manager was far from happy over Liverpool's third goal. Asked if he felt the keeper had dived too late to stop Robbie Fowler's shot, he replied curtly: "He has just about hit the deck now." And there was criticism for Bosnich over both goals in a 2-0 defeat by QPR, with McGrath regarded as his partner-in-crime for the first. "I understand there was a call for McGrath to leave the ball for the first goal," said Atkinson. "But the golden rule is: When in doubt, clear it. The second goal? Well, Bosnich was stupid."

Villa's headlines over the next few months were devoted to Atkinson's sacking, the appointment of his successor Brian Little and the team's mini-revival under their new boss. Come January, though, Bozzie was thrust back into the spotlight over a challenge which left Tottenham's Jurgen Klinsmann pole-axed at Villa Park. Racing out of the penalty area, Bosnich arrived at the ball fractionally before the German striker and had no option but to try and head clear. Unfortunately he crashed into Klinsmann, initially with his hip and then with a trailing boot to put the Spurs star out of the game by the 26th minute.

Bad as it looked, the sickening collision was regarded as accidental, and a Dean Saunders goal gave Villa a deserved 1-0 win. But Bosnich did neither himself nor his team-mates any favours when he was sent off for a moment of madness in a late-season match against Leeds at Elland Road. Cautioned for time-wasting on the stroke of half-time, he unnecessarily became embroiled in a shoving match with Carlton Palmer five minutes from time and was sent off for a second bookable offence. As if that wasn't bad enough, Palmer fired past substitute Spink in the last minute to condemn Villa to a 1-0 defeat. A consequent one-match suspension meant Bozzie missed the final game at Norwich, where Villa secured the point they required for top-flight survival, but the adversity of a relegation battle at least added to his experience. It also laid the foundations for what would be his – and Villa's – most successful Premiership season.

Little's team were awesome throughout 1995-96, winning the League Cup, reaching the FA Cup semi-finals and finishing fourth in the league – and Bosnich was one of only two players, along with Alan Wright, to start in all 51 games. He didn't quite make it as an "ever-present", being substituted by Spink in a 4-1 home victory over Coventry City because of a hamstring strain, but by now there was no question that he had well and truly established himself as the club's No. 1 goalkeeper. Not that any confirmation of his seniority were required, but it was provided when Spink ended a marvellous 19-year association with Villa by joining neighbours West Bromwich Albion in January. From now on, Bosnich's rival was Michael Oakes.

While Bozzie savoured his second cup-winners' medal in just under two years, his most satisfying afternoon's work was arguably against Manchester United – and we're not talking about the blistering 3-1 opening-day victory at Villa Park. The return fixture fell on Saturday 13th January, the Aussie's 24th birthday, and he celebrated by keeping a clean sheet in a goalless draw. In fairness, he was so well protected by a back three of Gareth Southgate, Paul McGrath and Ugo Ehiogu that he had to make only one serious save, from Ryan Giggs. But, not for the first time in his career, he left United boss Alex Ferguson frustrated.

It was Bosnich who experienced frustration at the start of the following campaign, knee problems restricting him to just a single appearance on the bench in the opening 10 games. And when he finally stepped into the side, it was in the most controversial of circumstances. Constantly barracked by Tottenham supporters over his challenge on Klinsmann two seasons earlier, he kept his cool until deep into the second half, when the latest round of chants about the striker prompted an unbelievable reaction. Holding a finger of his right hand above his lip to denote an Adolf Hitler moustache, he produced a Nazi salute with his left. It was intended as a humorous retort, bearing in mind that Klinsmann was German, but it was also a deeply offensive gesture to Spurs' large Jewish following.

To make matters worse, the act of stupidity was captured by photographers and splashed across both front and back pages of the Sunday papers. Bosnich and manager Little were also interviewed by the police after the game and it was clear the 'keeper was in big trouble. If he didn't immediately appreciate the seriousness of what he had done, it was brought home to him as Villa's coach headed back to Birmingham that evening. BBC Radio Five Live's Six-o-Six phone-in programme was deluged with calls about the incident, leaving Bozzie so upset that he broke his manager's curfew on mobile phones on the coach to make his own call to the programme to publicly apologise and express amazement that an action intended as a joke had proved to be so insulting.

"I'm a bit distraught, listening to those calls," he told Six-o-Six presenter David Mellor. "I'm under a few constraints because I'm on the team bus and I shouldn't really be using the mobile. But it's a sad reflection on society when something done in ignorance, as no more of a joke, should have been taken out of all proportion. I'm so, so sorry. I didn't mean to offend anyone and it's so sad that people want to string someone up over something like that.

"I came from Australia to play in England believing a big part of the game was the banter between players and the fans but it seems this is no longer the case. I know Spurs fans lost people in the war but I also lost people in the more recent war in Yugoslavia. I did something meaningless and a lot of the crowd seemed to be laughing but it looks like I got it wrong."

So determined was he to make amends for his insensitive

Basil Fawlty-type action that he even paid a personal visit to Tottenham chairman Alan Sugar to apologise. All the same, the issue dominated the headlines for more than a month before Bosnich faced his punishment at an FA hearing. He was fined £1,000 after the 80-minute enquiry as well as being severely censured and warned about his future conduct. In effect, the FA panel issued little more than a rap on the knuckles after concluding what the player had insisted all along – that his Nazi salute had been made in total innocence.

The Metropolitan Police accepted his explanation, too, deciding to take no further action, while Bosnich also escaped a suspension, although he still ended up missing seven more matches after suffering a recurrence of his knee ligament damage in a 1-0 defeat at Sunderland on the first weekend of November. He eventually returned for the 5-0 romp at home to Wimbledon on the Sunday before Christmas, which was tough on his understudy Michael Oakes, who had just kept three consecutive clean sheets – and Little must have wondered if he had made the right decision when two second-half Bozzie blunders presented Gianfranco Zola with the gift goals which gave Chelsea a 2-0 Boxing Day win at Villa Park.

Thankfully, that was a rare off-day, and Bosnich was largely in fine form until his infamous walk-out at Derby in April. His manager described it as "not the kind of behaviour I expect from a senior professional," and gave a succinct version of what had happened. "I picked the team, Mark wasn't in it and left the ground," he said. "There wasn't any conversation. I just got a message that he wasn't here any more."

Not for the first time, the 'keeper was forced to own up to his petulance. Although his apology to Little didn't prevent him from being dropped for the following match against Tottenham, which marked the 100th anniversary of Villa Park, he was recalled for the last two games as Villa secured fifth place and European qualification.

That summer, he even scored a penalty rather than saving one, netting his first professional goal in Australia's 13-0 romp against the Solomon Islands in Sydney, and he enjoyed another largely successful campaign in 1997-98. Despite kicking off with four straight defeats – the worst start in the club's history – Villa were transformed from relegation candidates to UEFA Cup qualifiers after John Gregory had succeeded Little as manager in February, and Bosnich played in all but nine of the team's 51 league and cup matches. Although his country missed out on the World Cup finals in France, there was a strong consensus of opinion that, had he been born in this country, he would have been a contender for the England team.

Sadly, his time as a Villa player was drawing to a close. His contract was due to expire 12 months later and he was reluctant to commit himself to the club for a further period, although he indicated on the opening day at Goodison Park that he intended to go out on a high note. He made another of his famous penalty saves that afternoon, parrying John Collins' spot-kick at the foot of his right-hand post and later waving triumphantly to Everton supporters after Villa had forced a goalless draw. It was a typical piece of Bosnich bravado, as Gregory happily acknowledged. "As soon as he saved the penalty, he started to antagonise everyone", said the manager, "including everyone on the bench!"

But uncertainty over his future, combined with shoulder and foot injuries, restricted him to 17 appearances that season before he followed his pal Dwight Yorke to Manchester United, moving to Old Trafford on a free transfer under the Bosman ruling.

Bosnich and Yorke had been close buddies ever since the Australian's arrival in the Midlands, although their friendship became a subject of ridicule just after Yorke's departure when *The Sun* ran a front-page story about them dressing up in women's clothes and getting up to all sorts of antics with a couple of young girls. The duo had even made a video of the sex party, which had found its way into the paper's possession, so there was no point in them denying what had taken place.

In fairness, no crime had been committed and by the time the media convened to preview the UEFA Cup tie against Stromsgodset not long afterwards, the unsavoury revelations had been pretty much forgotten. Our questions to John Gregory were confined purely to the task facing Villa in Scandinavia and he told us he had taken the precaution of having the opposition watched a couple of times because they were an unknown quantity. It was only natural, then, that he should be asked whether the Norwegians had been over here to check out Villa's strengths and weaknesses.

"Not as far as I'm aware," he replied. "But they did ask for a video." A wicked grin crossed his face before he added: "We sent 'em the one of Yorkie and Bozzie!"

MARK BOSNICH - CAREER STATS

BORN:	Fairfield, New South Wales
DATE OF BIRTH:	January 13 1972
JOINED VILLA:	December 1989
VILLA LEAGUE APPS:	179
GOALS:	0
VILLA CUP APPS:	49
GOALS	0
INT. CAPS (Australia):	22
GOALS:	1

1992-1995

Dean Saunders

The hypnotic drone of the small plane's twin engines was the only sound inside the dimly-lit cabin as we headed back from Spain in the early hours of Saturday morning. A few hours earlier, Villa had beaten Atletico Madrid on penalties in a pre-season tournament in the coastal town of Ferrol and most of the players were dozing as we approached the end of the flight home.

Their fatigue was understandable. We had flown out of Birmingham at 8am the previous day and it would be 20 hours later by the time we landed back on home soil. With everyone around me apparently asleep, it seemed the perfect opportunity to write my match report – until I felt something flick across the back of the head. Glancing behind me, I noticed that everyone had their eyes closed, so I presumed it had been an insect and continued tapping away at the laptop. Then I was hit once more, then again, and realised that the offending items were salted peanuts.

This time, when I looked around, the culprits revealed themselves. A couple of rows back, on the other side of the aisle, Dean Saunders and Dalian Atkinson were struggling to suppress their laughter. On the pitch, they were a deadly striking duo; off it, they were as mischievous as a couple of naughty schoolboys. And as the only other passenger in the land of consciousness, they had chosen me for target practice.

The incident would have amused manager Ron Atkinson, who was sound asleep on the row in front. It wouldn't have surprised him, either, although there was a time when it might have done. Less than two years earlier, he had been drawn to a footballer's goalscoring ability without really appreciating that he was also signing one of the most engaging personalities ever to pull on a claret and blue shirt.

Few players in Villa's history have endeared themselves to supporters as quickly as Dean Saunders did. He was at the club for less than three years but always headed the goal charts – and invariably had a smile on his face.

"Before I met him, I got the impression he was a very quiet personality, even dour," admitted Big Ron not long after signing Deano for a club record £2.3m. "But he is a bubbly, lively character, a real bundle of laughs and I love people like that. It's infectious and rubs off on other people."

What the Villa boss was saying, effectively, was that he had signed a striker and found a soul mate, a man very much after his own heart. Big Ron always enjoyed being surrounded by people with spirit and zest, and Dean Saunders fitted the bill perfectly. A darting, menacing striker on the pitch, he was also a social charmer. His cheeky grin and lilting Welsh accent endeared him immediately to anyone who met him and the Villa fans loved him, too. It wasn't long after he signed that the PA system at Villa Park first blasted out *Geno*, the record which had been a hit for *Dexy's Midnight Runners*. Holte Enders quickly came up with their own take on the lyrics.

"Oh-oh, Dean-o!" they sang, and if it was nowhere near as melodic as the choirs of the Welsh valleys, it was sweet music to the ears of a player who followed in the footsteps of others who had worn Villa's famous No. 9 shirt with distinction, men such as Gerry Hitchens, Tony Hateley, Andy Lochhead, Andy Gray and Peter Withe.

Saunders took the first step towards his place alongside

those Holte End heroes when he signed for Villa in September 1992, although he had been on Atkinson's shopping list long before then. As far back as July, the Villa boss had gone public about his interest, returning from a holiday in Tenerife to reveal that his striking targets for the launch of the Premier League were Saunders and his Wales international colleague Mark Hughes. In truth, the man Atkinson really wanted was England striker Alan Shearer, then a Southampton player. He was sure, however, that the Saints' £4m asking price meant Shearer would end up at Anfield or Old Trafford, which was why he was weighing up the strengths of players likely to become surplus to the needs of Liverpool and Manchester United.

One thing was certain. Ron wasn't about to be rushed. "It's no secret we want a new striker if we can get one, but only if it's the right one," he told the *Sunday Mercury*. "Otherwise we'll go into the season with what we've got." Which is exactly what Villa did, although his assumption that his number one target was destined for one of the Red giants of the North West proved to be considerably wide of the mark. Shearer ended up signing for Blackburn Rovers for £3.6m.

Not that Atkinson was too concerned about the England striker's movements when he finally landed Saunders. Villa's early form in the new league had been patchy to say the least, comprising two wins, three draws (in each of the opening three games) and two defeats, and the manager knew he needed a prolific marksman alongside Dalian Atkinson if his team were to rise above mid-table mediocrity. He even took the unusual step of broadcasting a message to supporters before a 3-0 victory over Crystal Palace on Saturday 5th September that "every effort" would be made to bring Saunders to Villa Park in time for the following weekend's match at Leeds United.

The hope was that, after considerable wrangling between the clubs over the price, Villa chairman Doug Ellis and Liverpool chief executive Peter Robinson would iron out any differences over the deal while in London together on the Monday after the Palace victory, and that the deal would go through by Thursday.

In the event, it was mid-morning on Wednesday when Ric George, a football writer on the *Liverpool Echo*, called me with the most concise of messages: "Saunders is coming to Villa," he said. "The fee is £2.3m. I don't have anything more just yet, but you can go ahead and write it."

Ric and I had known each other for some time and we occasionally shared information which was mutually beneficial to our respective papers, so I knew this was no idle speculation. He was closer to the Anfield club than any other reporter at that time so I knew the information had come from a good source. Along with the Liverpool evening paper, the *Birmingham Mail* was first to announce that Villa had just made a record signing.

A year earlier, Liverpool had also made Saunders their most expensive purchase, paying a British record £2.9m to persuade Derby County to part with his services, and he scored 23 goals for the Merseysiders as well as helping them to win the FA Cup. Yet he somehow never fitted the bill for manager Graeme Souness, and when Liverpool needed to raise money for team strengthening it was decided that Saunders could leave.

That in itself was something of a compliment, because he was clearly the player who could command the highest fee. And Ron Atkinson certainly had no misgivings over breaking Villa's transfer record for the third time in 14 months, following the acquisition of Dalian Atkinson (£1.6m) and full-back Earl Barrett (£1.7m).

"I'm as excited over this signing as any I have made in my career," the manager enthused. "Dean's a predator, the best in the business when it comes to scoring goals. He's also a quick and tireless worker. He will wear the No. 9 shirt. He won't be asked to take on different roles, his job is simply to attack the goal."

Understandably, the manager was in equally upbeat mood as

he prepared for Villa's next match – and Saunders' debut – at Elland Road. Leeds had been champions the previous season and reporters asked the inevitable question: Could Villa make a serious challenge for the title? The answer was straight from the book of Atkinson one-liners:

"We would have had a shot at the title even if we had signed Dean Martin, never mind Dean Saunders!"

Big Ron also revealed the fact that his new signing had done something unheard of in the modern game, accepting a massive pay cut for the privilege of continuing his career in claret and blue rather than in red.

"I'm not sure many other players would have moved," said the Villa boss. "He could have sat there in the reserves, or whatever, and seen out his contract. But he is what I call an old-fashioned player who wants to play. He has taken a drop in wages of almost 50 per cent. I think he wants to be appreciated. I told him he can be the king here, whereas at Liverpool he was just one of a number."

Saunders went some way to justifying that glowing testimonial with an encouraging debut in a 1-1 draw at Elland Road, and would have opened his goal account but for an offside flag. On reflection, it's almost as if fate decreed that he should wait until the following Saturday to register his first goal in claret and blue – it was the day Liverpool came to Villa Park!

A former Villa player opened the scoring, Mark Walters volleying Liverpool in front in the 43rd minute and that should really have been the Merseysiders' second goal, Ronny Rosenthal having earlier contrived to hit the bar when facing an open target after he had taken the ball past 'keeper Nigel Spink.

That incredible miss – which still raises a chuckle down Witton way – persuaded Ron Atkinson it might be Villa's day, despite a generally poor first-half performance from his players. The new boy was obviously on the same wavelength. A minute after Walters' goal, Garry Parker's fine pass found Steve Froggatt on the left and the young winger's cross was swept home at close range by a jubilant Saunders.

If scoring in front of Liverpool's supporters gave him immense satisfaction, it was merely a prelude to his unbridled delight when his 66th-minute shot went through goalkeeper David James's legs for his first goal at the Holte End. He might have had a hat-trick, too, when another effort struck the angle of post and bar, but he wasn't complaining. Two goals in a 4-2 victory over the club who had just shown him the door made it a home debut to savour. Typically, he was in cheeky mood afterwards.

"All season I have been getting into similar situations," he said. "But the ball has either hit the goalkeeper or the post. Today they both went through the goalkeeper's legs!"

Dalian Atkinson was also on target that afternoon and it was very much the start of a beautiful friendship for the *Deadly Duo*. Over the course of the next seven weeks, there was simply no stopping them as they created havoc among opposition defences.

Seven days after the demolition of Liverpool, it was again a case of Saunders two, Atkinson one – goals, that is – in a 3-2 success at Middlesbrough. A week later, it was exactly the same scoreline, and the same scorers, against Wimbledon at Selhurst Park, although on that occasion Deano's brace took a back seat to the single contribution from Dalian. The burly striker brushed aside four challenges in an amazing run from inside his own half before looking up briefly, spotting Hans Segers off his line and chipping craftily over the goalkeeper and into the net. There have been numerous other candidates down the years, but most Villa supporters still rank that one as the club's best Premiership goal.

At the time, it took the team's goal haul to an impressive 10 in three league games, nine of them coming from Saunders and Atkinson, and while such an incredible ratio was obviously impossible to maintain, the duo continued to score on a regular basis as their team steadily climbed the table.

They clearly had no respect for reputations, either. Saunders hit the goal which secured a 1-0 win over Manchester United in the League Cup; ten days later Atkinson followed suit as Villa beat United by the same scoreline in a league match. In between times, they netted one each in a 2-0 victory over third-placed Queens Park Rangers. No wonder their manager drooled: "Dean Saunders is brilliant. He is simply the best striker in the league for my money – and I believe there's an awful lot more to come from Dalian."

As it happened, there wasn't a great deal more to come from Deano's partner that season. Atkinson hit both goals in a 2-1 win at Sheffield Wednesday in early December, taking him to 13 in 22 league and cup games, but then hardly played for the next four months because of a stomach injury. He returned to action as Villa went top with a 1-0 win at Nottingham Forest in April but didn't manage to add to his goal tally for the remainder of the season.

That win at the City Ground wasn't the first time Villa had climbed to the Premiership summit. They had achieved the feat in mid-January with a 5-1 thrashing of Middlesbrough, when Saunders was among the scorers. But even that didn't give Deano quite the same sense of satisfaction as the goal he had scored eight days earlier. His home debut brace against Liverpool in September had been something special, but scoring in front of the Kop in January was even better – particularly as it was the winner after Garry Parker's strike had cancelled out a first half John Barnes goal.

Goalkeeper Nigel Spink's long clearance was headed on by Dwight Yorke, and Saunders brushed off the challenge of Danish defender Torben Piechnik to send a left-foot drive past goalkeeper Mike Hooper and reduce the Kop to a stunned silence.

It was Villa's first win at Anfield since 1977, and it had been 40 years since their previous double over Liverpool. Back then, as Andy Colquhoun put it in the *Birmingham Post*: 'Ron Atkinson was wearing short trousers and Doug Ellis was a million short of his first million.' Now, Atkinson relished the moment in the visitors' dug-out, while Ellis watched contentedly from the Anfield directors' box.

Neither manager nor chairman, though, could have been as ecstatic as the man who made it happen – even if Deano tried to play down his obvious delight afterwards. "I wondered what it would be like to score the winner here and I'm very happy I did," he told reporters. "But the result was more important than anything else. I will get all the headlines, I suppose, and the lads at the back won't get a mention. But I was watching from the halfway line when all those corners were raining in towards the end and all I could see was our lads heading the ball out. In the past, I don't think I have played in a visiting team who have even scored at Anfield – let alone won a game!"

Victory at Anfield was undoubtedly the pinnacle of Saunders' first season in claret and blue but there were plenty of other highlights as he finished his debut campaign as the club's leading scorer.

His spot-kick winner at home to Arsenal, for instance, was Villa's first Premier League penalty conversion, delivered with pace and precision past goalkeeper David Seaman after Dwight Yorke had been sent sprawling by David O'Leary. Then he was on target twice in a 3-0 FA Cup replay victory at Bristol Rovers, giving his manager the last laugh after Atkinson had been referred to as "Fat Ron" by Rovers' outspoken boss Malcolm Allison during the build-up to the third-round tie.

And he came up with a super strike which some Villa folk would put ahead of Atkinson's solo run and chip as the club's best goal of the Premiership era. There were actually two contenders for the crown that February afternoon against Ipswich Town at Villa Park, Yorke having opened the scoring with a fine diving header following defence-splitting passes from Steve Froggatt and Garry Parker and a superb Steve Staunton centre. But Deano's effort 10 minutes later was more memorable because of its sheer audacity.

Receiving a pass from Ray Houghton, the Welsh wizard hit an exquisite volley from almost 40 yards, the ball drifting over goalkeeper Clive Baker and just under the bar. "Sensational" was Ron Atkinson's verdict, while even Ipswich boss Mick McGiven was gracious enough to concede that the goal on its own was worth the price of admission. Inevitably, there was a question, too, for the scorer about his intention when the ball left his boot. "Of course I meant it," he replied. "I looked up and spotted that the 'keeper was off his line."

Unfortunately, it was a goal which would have to keep Saunders going through a drought which lay just around the corner, a barren spell which would last 11 matches before he brought it to an end with the equaliser in a home win over Manchester City. Even during his lean period, however, he was always threatening, hitting the post in four consecutive games as well as having what looked a perfectly good effort disallowed when the ball appeared to be over the line in a goalless draw against Tottenham Hotspur.

Having gone more than a thousand minutes without scoring, Deano's header against City could not have been more welcome and the 3-1 result meant his first-ever involvement with a team challenging for the league title might still end successfully. The notion was destroyed, sadly, by a 3-0 drubbing the following Wednesday at the hands of a Blackburn Rovers side inspired by Villa legend Gordon Cowans, and a 1-0 home defeat by relegation-threatened Oldham Athletic four days later confirmed that Villa would have to settle for the runners-up spot behind Manchester United.

Even so, it had been a season in which Saunders began to feel appreciated again after his unhappy episode at Liverpool, even if he happened to be one of the first victims of the Premier League's 'dubious goals' committee. To all intents and purposes, he finished his debut campaign with a total of 17 goals but the figure was reduced to 16 after the newly-formed committee deemed that his acrobatic scissor-kick in a 3-1 home win over Sheffield United should be regarded as a Chris Kamara own goal. Given the fact that Saunders' shot had beaten goalkeeper Alan Kelly and was going in anyway, it was a strange and, indeed, unjust decision.

We can only presume that the newly-formed panel had to come up with something to justify their existence, and the man the ball struck on its way into the net would happily give the goal back to its rightful scorer. "I remember it well," says Kamara. "To be honest, I didn't realise the goal had been taken away from Dean. The ball just happened to hit me as it was going in; there was nothing I could have done to stop it. I can't understand why it was considered an own goal. Then again, the Dubious Goals Panel have come up with some dubious decisions over the years!"

Not that it unduly worried either Saunders or Villa as the 1993-94 season opened with an emphatic 4-1 home win over Queens Park Rangers, although the goal the Welsh wizard scored that day was one of only three he netted on home soil before Christmas, one of his others helping to complete a 2-0 aggregate victory over neighbours Birmingham City in the League Cup. He was no more prolific on his travels either, although one of his three away strikes was one of his most important yet in claret and blue. Or, at least, it should have been. His clinical 79th-minute finish in the first leg of a second round UEFA Cup tie against Deportivo La Coruna provided Villa with a vital away goal and even though the Spanish side grabbed a late equaliser, hopes were high that Villa would progress to round three. It wasn't to be. At Villa Park two weeks later, the team's naivety in the business of European competition was exposed as they slipped to a 1-0 defeat.

If Saunders was frequently firing blanks during the first half of the season, at least his manager never lost faith in him. Ron Atkinson made it clear he would wield the axe if necessary but after Deano had squandered a potential hat-trick in a 2-2 draw against QPR at Loftus Road, the boss refused to be critical. It was the striker's eighth game without scoring since his goal in Spain, but Atkinson said afterwards: "His last two performances have been his best of the season. He is setting up chances, making the runs and doing the right things."

Always a player who responded to an arm around his shoulder, Saunders' response was to end his drought against Sheffield Wednesday four days later, and while his scoring didn't exactly become prolific, at least he maintained a steady output of important goals from that juncture. There was the winner in a 2-1 success at Norwich City as Villa ended 1993 with a superb display of attacking football; the penalty which sank battling Exeter City in the FA Cup; the goal which earned a draw at Chelsea – and then one of the hat-tricks which have been all too rare from Villa players during the Premiership years. All right, so Swindon Town offered pitiful resistance as Villa romped home 5-0; all right, so two of Saunders' treble were penalties. But that afternoon he became the first Villa player to score a Premier League hat-trick, and only five others have subsequently repeated the feat.

Yet given the choice, he would no doubt have saved those goals for the next three games, in which Villa lost 3-1 at Tranmere Rovers in the first leg of the League Cup semi-final, went down 1-0 at Bolton Wanderers in the fifth round of the FA Cup and were held to a goalless home draw by Manchester City on a night when Saunders went on as a 72nd-minute substitute, earned a penalty when he was brought down by Richard Edghill – and then sent the kick two yards off target.

The usually effervescent Dean Saunders was a picture of

despair as snow added to the wind-chill factor to make it a thoroughly miserable February night. But a beaming smile was back on his face the following Sunday as he played a significant part in a match many supporters regard as the best to have taken place at Villa Park during the Premiership era.

The prospect of Saunders and his pals getting to Wembley had seemed remote in the extreme when Tranmere went three-up in the first leg of the League Cup semi-final, and although Dalian Atkinson's late volley at Prenton Park had offered a glimmer of hope, the odds were still stacked heavily in Rovers' favour before kick-off in the return match.

But Saunders did all that was expected of him that afternoon. His 19th-minute goal offered Villa a platform for their recovery and after the tie had finished 4-4 on aggregate, he was the first to step forward in one of the most dramatic penalty shoot-outs you will ever see. He may have missed five days earlier but this one, in a far more pressurised situation, was despatched with all the confidence of a man destined for his second cup final in less than two years.

Ultimately, it was left to Mark Bosnich to assume the role of hero, the goalkeeper saving three of Tranmere's kicks as Villa won an unbearably tense shoot-out to clinch their place at Wembley, but Saunders' contribution in settling Villa nerves, both in normal time and in the penalty competition, should not be underestimated.

Neither should his contribution to a cup final in which Villa were expected to be on the receiving end of a real thumping. Atkinson's men drew 1-1 at Tottenham immediately after their semi-final victory and then won 1-0 at Coventry City, before embarking on a run of three straight defeats at the hands of Ipswich, Leeds and Oldham, who were 20th in the table when they arrived at Villa Park and were still in 20th position when they left, despite a 2-1 win which resulted in Villa's players being jeered by a pitifully low crowd of 21,214.

The omens for Wembley eight days later were far from encouraging, as Mike Ward observed in the *Birmingham Post*. 'It appears,' he wrote, 'that only a double puncture to the team bus can save Aston Villa from the humiliation Manchester United have in store for them at the end of the M1 motorway next Sunday.'

Saunders was feeling the strain more than most. Having failed to score in any of the five Premiership games since the semi-final, he was in far from his usual buoyant mood in the days leading up the final. But, not for the first time in his career, you wouldn't have guessed he had a care in the world as the big stage brought the best out of him. He charmed the claret and blue end of Wembley, creating the opening goal for his strike partner Atkinson and netting another two himself in the 3-1 triumph over United.

Those three crucial moments encompassed the many facets of Deano's game. His deft flick, which let in Atkinson for the opening goal on 25 minutes, was one a cultured midfielder would have been proud of. The manner in which he stuck out his left leg to divert Tony Daley's free-kick inside the near post for the second goal was opportunism at its finest. His late penalty, after Andrei Kanchelskis had been sent off for handling an Atkinson shot on the line, was all about determination as he thumped his kick past goalkeeper Les Sealey to secure victory. The final was the 500th game of his career and he was intent on celebrating in style as he became only the second Villa player, following Peter McParland in 1957, to score twice in a Wembley final.

Perhaps he overdid the celebrations. He was on target just once more – in a 4-1 defeat at Southampton – although he missed three of Villa's remaining nine games through injury. And his single strike was enough to make him the club's 16-goal leading scorer for the second consecutive season, one ahead of Atkinson.

If headlines about Saunders were thin on the ground in those closing weeks of the campaign, though, he was thrust into the spotlight with a vengeance in late May and early June.

Five days before joining Villa, he had been involved in a challenge with Chelsea's Paul Elliott which ended the defender's career. Now he was being sued for compensation. Deano, accustomed to appearing in front of thousands of supporters on the football stage, was suddenly the centre of attention in a courtroom in a case which lasted for nine days and attracted widespread media coverage.

In normal circumstances, it would have been of only passing interest to the *Birmingham Evening Mail*, because Saunders had been playing for Liverpool at the time of the incident. But he was now Villa's star player, while Elliott also had a claret and blue connection, having played for the club during the late 1980s.

My editor decided I should attend the opening day of the proceedings at London's Royal Court of Justice and I spoke briefly to Dean outside court before the hearing began. He certainly didn't give the impression of being guilty of a career-ending challenge and while he was sorry that Elliott was no longer able to earn a living from football, he was adamant it had been an accident. Deano's confidence was reflected by the relaxed manner in which he sat through early stages of the hearing, listening to various former players and referees as they gave their opinions on the unfortunate tackle.

Given the huge amount of money involved – Elliott was seeking compensation of around £500,000 – it was a deadly serious business, though not without its lighter moments. All around the chamber, there was the sort of sombre mood you associate with court proceedings, but in the middle of the chamber there was a table which accommodated a green baize *Subbuteo* pitch, complete with goals, corner flags and 22 miniature figures in red and blue. It was all very surreal as we were given an 'action replay' of what had happened at Anfield, courtesy of those perfectly-balanced flick-to-kick plastic footballers. Deano certainly found it amusing as he frequently looked across the courtroom at me with raised eyebrows or his trademark grin and wink.

Even so, he must have been deeply concerned about the possible financial implications of the case before the judge, Lord Justice Drake, ruled in his favour. If he had been sent off for the challenge, maybe it would have been a different story but, as the court heard, he hadn't even received a caution. In fact, a free-kick had been awarded to Liverpool. Outside the court after the verdict had been delivered, Dean stood smiling in front of TV cameras and press photographers, happily agreeing to requests for the 'thumbs-up' picture which appeared in most of the following day's newspapers.

It had been one of the most trying periods of his life but he had come up with the right result – and the experience stood him in good stead for the remainder of his career.

"My reputation was dragged through the mud and after that experience I can go through anything in football," he said a few weeks later, and it was perhaps as well. The 1994-95 season was the least successful of Villa's Premiership campaigns and they only avoided relegation on the final day, but there's no doubt that Saunders' 15 league goals played a significant part in their survival.

There was no hint, during the first few weeks of the campaign, that the team would struggle like they did. Three draws, two wins and three Saunders goals suggested that further success was on the horizon. Unfortunately, Deano's supply line ran dry and he scored only twice more over the course of the next 15 games as Villa slid down the table and went out of the UEFA Cup. When he finally snapped back to his best, it was too late to save his manager from the sack.

Villa looked set to end a dismal run of eight games without a win when Saunders' first brace of the season helped to establish a 3-1 lead by the 50th minute of the game against Villa's bogey side Wimbledon at Selhurst Park. Even the handicap of being down to 10 men following Andy Townsend's sending-off seemed to present no real problem as Deano fired home his second goal, and for 15 minutes afterwards we wondered just why Villa were occupying 19th place in the table.

The final 25 minutes revealed the answer as 3-1 became 3-4 to leave the side with just one point from a possible 27. It was rough on Villa, who had actually been playing some decent football during their depressing run, but it was one defeat too many for Big Ron. He was asked to attend a board meeting the following day and was informed that his services were no longer required.

As the wheels were set in motion on the bitter saga which would bring former Holte End favourite Brian Little from Leicester City as Atkinson's successor, Villa supporters could have been excused for wondering why the club didn't simply give the job to the man who assumed a caretaker role. Jim Barron was in charge for just one match but a dramatic victory over Tottenham meant he could boast a 100 per cent record!

The match at White Hart Lane came 10 days after the fateful night at Selhurst Park and at one stage it looked as if Villa were about to self-destruct in the capital yet again. Three-up inside half-an-hour, their cosy advantage was obliterated by the 71st minute. Villa stood firm under intense pressure, though, and three minutes into stoppage time Saunders brushed aside Gary Mabbutt's challenge to lash home the winner.

Having scored three times in two games under Atkinson and then Barron, Deano was unable to maintain his scoring form once Little arrived and we had had to wait until New Year's Eve, and a 2-2 draw at Manchester City, for his next goal.

Then, typically, he was on target eight times in nine games during January and February, netting five in three consecutive matches against Wimbledon, Sheffield Wednesday and Leicester City. Despite scoring twice against the Dons he was overshadowed by Tommy Johnson's hat-trick, but his brace at Hillsborough seven days later was accompanied by a brilliant performance. My 15-year-old daughter, who had become a firm Deano fan by that stage, asked before I set out for Yorkshire if I would get his autograph for her – even though he had already signed it for her in person on a couple of occasions. He chuckled when I told him she wanted his signature yet again. This time, without even writing his name, he came up with an unusual autograph which reflected his afternoon's endeavours – 'To Helen, 2 today!'

An impressive run of league results since Christmas had lifted Villa into ninth in the table by that stage and such was the team's resurgence under Little that there was even talk about European qualification for the third consecutive year. Saunders, meanwhile, was talking about reaching the magical 20-goal mark, but both the team's and the striker's lofty ambitions turned out to be pipedreams.

Saunders opened the scoring after just eight minutes against Leicester the following Wednesday and by the 67th minute, an on-song Villa outfit led 4-1. But Little's former team bounced back to force a 4-4 draw. From that juncture, survival was top of the Villa agenda.

They would win only twice in the final dozen games, while Saunders would never score again in a Villa shirt. Even so, his 17-goal total made him the club's leading marksman for the third consecutive season, a fact which didn't go unnoticed both here and abroad. As early as January, Villa had turned down a couple of bids from Everton, with Little insisting: "Dean's not for sale. He's one of those players I don't want to lose."

Sadly, that's not the way it turned out. Saunders had a clause in his contract allowing him to move abroad if the price was right and in July he signed for Turkish giants Galatasaray, although he told me just before heading off to Istanbul that he would happily return to Villa at the end of his contract if the opportunity were to present itself. In the event, he came back with Nottingham Forest two seasons later and again with newly-promoted Bradford City in 1999.

Most former players are automatically booed on their return to the club, but not Deano. He was given a rousing reception on both occasions, as he has been on subsequent visits in a coaching role for the opposition. Lifelong Villa supporter Richard Whitehead has a plausible theory for his enduring popularity. "Maybe it's because he sprinkled a little stardust over Villa Park when he arrived," says Richard. "He had been a British record transfer little more than a year earlier and he turned a useful team into one that could, and perhaps should, have won the title."

Saunders had no thoughts about titles that afternoon with Bradford, who were more concerned with Premiership survival and whose ambition at Villa Park stretched no further than trying to hold on for a point. In those circumstances, there was never any prospect of him reproducing the exciting form which had made him such a firm favourite in claret and blue. Playing as a lone striker, he endured a fruitless 90 minutes against Villa's solid central defensive partnership of Gareth Southgate and Ugo Ehiogu as Dion Dublin's 71st-minute goal clinched a 1-0 home win.

Afterwards he joked: "I think Ugo did more attacking than me!" Fine player that he was, Dean Saunders could never be accused of taking himself too seriously.

DEAN SAUNDERS - CAREER STATS

BORN:	Swansea
DATE OF BIRTH:	June 21 1964
JOINED VILLA:	September 1992
VILLA LEAGUE APPS:	112
GOALS:	37
VILLA CUP APPS:	32
GOALS:	12
INT. CAPS (Wales):	75
GOALS:	22

1993-1997

Andy Townsend

Andy Townsend had just one thought in his head when he joined Aston Villa. A single-minded individual, he was a footballer who knew exactly what he wanted. And that, quite simply, was to be a winner.

He was a seasoned professional by then and, as his 30th birthday passed, he must have wondered if the major honours were always destined to pass him by. After all, he had played in five semi-finals with three different clubs – and finished on the losing side every time.

But he couldn't possibly have known, when he switched from Stamford Bridge to Villa Park in July 1993, just how dramatically his fortunes were about to change. Where he had missed out on cup finals with Southampton, Norwich City and Chelsea, he would reach Wembley twice within the next three years. Better still, he would be on the winning side on both occasions. Best of all, he would be captain when Villa won the League Cup for the second time in three seasons.

Don't run away with the idea, though, that this is the story of what Aston Villa did for Andy Townsend. Anyone who watched the team on a regular basis during those glory years will tell you that Andy Townsend also did an awful lot for Villa. His midfield dominance and powerful runs – not to mention a few crucial goals – gave the side a vital edge they had previously lacked.

He also wore his heart on his sleeve whenever he stepped on

to a football pitch, a characteristic which sometimes landed him in trouble when referees took exception to his exuberant approach. He once served a six-match suspension, accumulated by a series of bookings plus a red card – and promptly earned himself another two-match ban by being sent off in his comeback match!

For all that, the plus points of his wholehearted approach far outweighed any occasional brushes with authority and he gave outstanding service to Villa before moving to Middlesbrough four years after his arrival in the Midlands. His switch to Teesside meant he dropped down a division, although he quickly made a point that at the age of 34, he still had a lot to offer, helping Boro back to the Premiership at the first time of asking. That would have come as no surprise at all to the man who brought him to Villa Park.

One of Ron Atkinson's first tasks following his appointment as manager in the summer of 1991 had been to sanction the departure of David Platt to Italian club Bari for £5.5m. It was a sum which represented a huge profit to Villa, who had paid a mere £200,000 to bring Platt from Crewe Alexandra. But while Big Ron had certainly not lacked conviction in his transfer dealings in the intervening two years, he had not come up with anyone capable of emulating the England international.

"Since David Platt left the club, we haven't had someone who can drive and thrust from midfield," he said at the time. "Andy Townsend has got that ability. He has tremendous energy, gets up and down the field and is competitive. He also scored nine goals last season and I would be looking for him to at least equal that figure."

In the latter respect, Townsend was a disappointment. It took him three seasons to score nine goals for Villa and by the time he moved on, his tally stood at only 11. But there were some crucial strikes among that modest total, and there can be no argument about the fact that he delivered in every other aspect of his game.

The manager readily acknowledged he was taking something of a gamble by paying £2.1m for a 30-year-old, admitting that if people had predicted the scenario 12 months earlier, he would have said they were "off their rocker."

Even so, Atkinson must have felt a warm glow of satisfaction as Townsend proved to be everything he was looking for with a storming debut in a 4-1 opening-day thrashing of Queens Park Rangers. In his match report in the *Birmingham Post*, Andy Colquhoun described the new signing as 'the big boy in the schoolyard kick-around. It is Townsend's greatest attribute,' he wrote. 'Shouldering tackles aside, stretching out for a concrete-solid tackle and generally playing bully in the midfield scrap.'

Such was the midfielder's desire for involvement, unfortunately, that he strained a hamstring during the midweek goalless draw at Sheffield Wednesday and missed the next three matches. He was back in the line-up, though, for a 1-0 win at Everton and then produced his first goal for the club in a 2-1 success at Ipswich Town as Villa's season started to gain momentum. It was a magnificent effort, too. Accepting Kevin Richardson's short pass from the right-hand touchline, he took a stride forward before unleashing a wickedly-bending 35-yard drive which flew past goalkeeper Craig Forrest and into the top corner for a 55th-minute winner.

His next goal was equally important, his left-foot shot from just outside the penalty area securing a 2-1 victory over Slovan Bratislava and progress to the second round of the UEFA Cup. And as if to underline his penchant for scoring when it really mattered, his other two goals during his debut season were also match-winners.

The first, against Arsenal at Highbury in November, brought a wry smile from manager Atkinson, who was honest enough to admit his team had "mugged" the Gunners after they snatched an unlikely 2-1 victory. Second best for most of the game, Villa appeared to be heading for certain defeat when Ian Wright fired Arsenal ahead just before the hour mark. A 74th-minute equaliser against the run of play from substitute Guy Whittingham appeared to have earned a point Villa scarcely deserved but there was better to come. In stoppage time, Dean Saunders chased a seemingly lost cause to retrieve the ball near the corner flag before crossing for Townsend to send a superb right-foot drive inside David Seaman's near post.

Townsend's other strike, this time with his left, sank Leeds United 1-0 at Villa Park in February and typified his resilience. His nose had been bleeding heavily following a blow from Jon Newsome's elbow and his arm had to be strapped after Brian Deane stepped on it but that wasn't about to stop him delivering a knockout blow of his own. A raking pass from Earl Barrett sent him bearing down on the visitors' goal and he ignored the discomfort from his nose and the pain from his arm to send a swerving shot past goalkeeper Mark Beeney. Villa's all-action commando had lost a couple of battles but had won the war – or, at least, the match. No wonder he was described by his boss as "tremendous".

As for the man himself, the winning goal at least helped him to see the funny side of his injuries. "I was caught flush in the nose but there wasn't any intent," he said. "When I was hit on the arm I thought: 'What's happening out here? What have I done to deserve this?' Thankfully it came right for us in the end. As for the goal, I was that knackered by the time I got the ball, I hardly had the strength to hit it!"

Townsend's total of four was slightly less than half the nine-goal figure Atkinson had hoped for, but his contribution to the team that season was immense and Villa invariably missed his driving force on the odd occasions he was ruled out by injury. Villa were far from a one-man team, but we had a classic example of his influence when a knee operation ruled him out of three matches before Christmas. During his absence, the team struggled to a 2-2 home draw against Sheffield Wednesday, went down 1-0 to Wimbledon at Villa Park and were comprehensively beaten by league-leaders Manchester United at Old Trafford. Maybe the latter result had an air of inevitability about it anyway, but he was sorely missed as five home points were squandered against the Owls and the Dons. When Townsend returned to action, significantly, Villa produced one of their finest displays of the season to beat Norwich City 2-1 at Carrow Road.

Thankfully, Andy was also available for every one of the team's League Cup-ties, and when Villa beat Manchester United 3-1 in the final at Wembley he was finally able to celebrate his first major honour. He revelled in the whole experience, too. During the week leading up to the final, he agreed to provide a daily column for the *Birmingham Evening Mail* and he approached the task with all the enthusiasm he would have put into a training session. Each day, when I called him at the hotel where the team were based, he dutifully recounted stories about his colleagues and what was happening in the build-up to the big game. He also related how he was keeping himself and his team-mates entertained in the evenings by strumming his guitar. But the best column of all was the one he wrote after the final, outlining his sheer delight at collecting a winners' medal after all those semi-final heartaches with his previous clubs. Mind you, there was a moment when he feared history was about to repeat itself.

"I'll never forget the first leg of our semi-final against Tranmere," he says. "We were three-down and although Dalian Atkinson smacked one in right at the end to give us a glimmer of hope, we knew it was still a tall order to reach the final. I don't think I've ever felt as low as I did that night. We'd been given the plum draw against Tranmere and before the match I thought we would just roll them over. When we lost 3-1 up there, I thought to myself: 'I can't believe what's happening to me. I'm destined to finish playing this game with bugger all to show for it.'

"But there was a lighter moment, as well. I was giving Dean Saunders guitar lessons at the time and he had his guitar with him. We were due for a day off the following day but Ron was fuming after the game and quite rightly wanted everyone in for training the next day. Dean lived in Manchester at the time and he wasn't at all happy about it. I'll never forget the sight of him storming across the car park, dragging his kit bag and his guitar behind him. He looked more like a disgruntled rock star than footballer!

"The second leg was an amazing afternoon, particularly the penalty shoot-out. At 4-4 my old Irish team-mate Liam O'Brien had the chance to win it for Tranmere and I knew how well he could strike a dead ball. When Mark Bosnich saved that one, I knew we were going to Wembley. Then Tony Daley made it 5-4 to us and when Bozzie saved the next one from Ian Nolan, it was an incredible feeling. All the players came back to my house for a party that night.

"By the time of the final, our league form was patchy, to say the least. Everyone fancied United to win at Wembley and quite rightly so. But Ron had a game plan. It was a big, bold decision to bring in young Graham Fenton and play five in midfield but it was one that paid off for us. It worked a treat on the day and it was a fantastic feeling to know I'd finally won something.

"Walking up the steps to get our medals, I spotted the Chelsea chairman Ken Bates. I'd got on pretty well with him during my time at Stamford Bridge but towards the end I felt let down because Chelsea were supposed to be signing so many brilliant players and it just hadn't happened. We'd had a few words and as I climbed those steps I thought I must remind him: 'This is why I left.' But as I got up to where he was sitting, the old sod looked the other way!

"But to be finally running around Wembley with a cup was a

magical feeling. One or two people often remind me what Chelsea went on to achieve but when I left they were very much in transition and I had no regrets about leaving them. I felt I had to get to another club if I wanted to win anything because I couldn't see it happening at Chelsea in the immediate future. This was a few years before their revolution, don't forget."

His departure from The Bridge hadn't gone down at all well with Chelsea supporters and in January, he had endured calls of 'Judas' from fans who hadn't forgiven him for joining Villa. It was bad enough that he was subjected to such vitriol, worse that it happened during a pre-match minute's silence in tribute to Sir Matt Busby, who had died that week. Indeed, one Chelsea supporter sitting just in front of the press box described the yells from the mindless minority as "a disgrace" and the episode was unpleasant in the extreme.

Such a hostile reception might have put lesser players off their game but Townsend's response was to produce his usual display of midfield strength in a 1-1 draw. If he was affected at all by the insult, he wasn't about to show it, either on the pitch or when he was interviewed afterwards. "The punters here have always been a bit colourful, so I expected some stick," he said. "But the Judas bit was a bit strong. I gave my heart and soul to this club when I was here. Really, though, I was more bothered that we didn't get the three points."

That typified Townsend's attitude. For him, the job in hand was all that mattered; everything else was peripheral. For example, despite undergoing knee surgery that summer, he declared his intention to be fit for the opening-day match at Everton, and was as good as his word. Unfortunately, he sometimes took his enthusiasm too far.

He was already facing a suspension for accumulating five early-season bookings when Villa headed to Selhurst Park to take on Wimbledon on Wednesday 9th November, and his red card in a 4-3 defeat by the Dons ensured that the ban was extended to six matches.

Atkinson was dismissed after that match, but to this day, Andy believes it was a hasty decision. "I was devastated when Ron was sacked," he says. "I was choked. I know we weren't getting results but I didn't think the situation needed radical surgery at that point. We were playing some decent football – Ron wouldn't have it any other way – and yes, we were under-achieving, but it wasn't because of anything Ron wasn't doing. He simply had world-class players who weren't performing well enough. The manager is always likely to face the bullet at times like that but the bottom line is that we weren't doing the business for him."

But it wasn't only Big Ron who was absent from the Villa scene. Supporters also saw nothing of Townsend until Boxing Day – and when he returned after his ban, he was sent off in his comeback match, a goalless draw against Arsenal at Highbury.

It seems almost incomprehensible that such an intelligent footballer should walk straight back into trouble after such a lengthy lay-off but it's fair to say that officialdom was as much to blame as Townsend. Referees were under orders to clamp down on offenders and in some cases they clearly took the punishment a step too far. The tackle on Wimbledon's Neal Ardley which got Townsend sent off, for instance, was considered by most observers to be worth no more than a yellow card, while at Highbury he was dismissed for a second bookable offence just past the hour mark. We were still getting used to the rule at the time and although the challenges both warranted a caution, the red card seemed harsh. Townsend, who was left facing a further two-match suspension, was not short on sympathy from Villa's new manager Brian Little.

"Andy is very disappointed," said the former Holte End favourite, "but such are the laws of the game now that even I would be getting booked – and anybody can tell you that was never the case for me when I was a player." Even Arsenal manager George Graham conceded: "Townsend didn't seem to deserve being sent off because there were a lot worse tackles in the game than his."

Frequent absences through suspension, and occasionally through injury, meant Townsend's goal output was even more modest than the previous season. This time he managed just two, one of them the winner against Middlesbrough when he captained the side in a third-round League Cup-tie, the other in a 3-1 defeat at Newcastle. His 25-yard left-footer at St. James's Park was a stunner, although it was also the first game Villa had lost when he had been on target.

It speaks volumes for his powerful midfield presence, though, that he was an automatic choice for the side whenever he was available and his vast experience was an invaluable asset throughout a problematic season, forming a solid central midfield partnership with Ian Taylor, who had signed from Sheffield Wednesday just before Christmas.

With the Premiership about to be reduced from 22 teams to 20 the following season, four teams had to be relegated from the top flight in 1995 and the tension around Villa Park was almost unbearable, as Little's men hovered just above the drop zone during the closing weeks. But Townsend and Taylor were instrumental in ensuring that Villa remained solid in midfield before safety was ensured on the final day. A headed goal from Townsend's Republic of Ireland team-mate Steve Staunton settled the nerves against Norwich City at Carrow Road, where Villa secured the point they required for safety, although results elsewhere meant they ultimately didn't need it.

All the same, the team's flirtation with relegation had been too close for comfort and that summer manager Brian Little splashed out more than £9m on three new players – Gareth Southgate, Savo Milosevic and Mark Draper. By then, Townsend was the only surviving midfielder from the Ron Atkinson era and with two of the new signings being midfielders, there was speculation his place would come under threat. After all, Little had offloaded several of the club's older players, including Kevin Richardson, Ray Houghton and Garry Parker and was clearly intent on developing a more youthful squad. His line-up at the start of 1995-96, in fact, was one of the youngest in the top flight – with two notable exceptions. One was Paul McGrath, now very much the veteran of the side at 36; the other was Andy Townsend, who had just turned 32. Little may have been building for the future but he also appreciated the value of an old head or two to help along his 'Young Ones'.

The manager's decision to keep faith with Townsend was astute in the extreme, for this was to be Villa's most successful Premiership campaign to date. Under the Ireland international's captaincy, they finished fourth in the table, reached the FA Cup semi-finals for the first time in 36 years – and won the League Cup for the second time in three seasons.

You somehow knew it was going to be a memorable season as temperatures nationwide soared to the high 80s. As Villa Park sweltered in tropical sunshine, the action against a youthful Manchester United outfit was equally hot. Three goals in the opening 36 minutes, from Ian Taylor, Mark Draper and a Dwight Yorke penalty made it the most blistering start imaginable for Townsend and his team-mates, United having to settle for a consolation goal seven minutes from time from a relatively unknown young man called David Beckham. On BBC's *Match of the Day* that night, former Liverpool star Alan Hansen made his infamous observation that "you'll never win anything with kids" and while he was proved spectacularly wrong as United's young upstarts went on to become champions, Villa's lofty finishing position proved that a touch of experience can come in handy, too.

After half-a-dozen matches, Little's men were third in the table, and immediately afterwards they took the first major step along the League Cup trail with a 6-0 thrashing of Peterborough

United. There was still the return match at London Road to come but a third-round place was assured. Even so, managers are notoriously cautious about any remarks they make in such circumstances and I'll never forget the moment Little took his seat for the post-match press conference. Before anyone else had the chance to ask a question, John Wragg of the *Daily Express* piped up: "Please don't say it's only half-time!"

The Villa boss smiled and acknowledged that, yes, it did look as if the tie was won, although he did have to confront a slightly contentious issue. Townsend had flicked the ball up for Draper to volley home the opening goal, prompting comparisons with Ernie Hunt's controversial goal for Coventry City 25 years earlier. Understandably, Little leapt to his captain's defence. "That free-kick was flicked up with two feet, which made it two touches, and illegal," he explained. "Townsend flicked the ball only once so there is no way that's illegal."

A few days later, as Villa surrendered their 100 per cent home record, it was very much a bittersweet occasion for Townsend. He opened the scoring against Nottingham Forest with a 69th-minute goal but his joy lasted barely two minutes. His next important contribution was to foul Lars Bohinen, which earned him a yellow card from referee Paul Danson, quickly followed by a red because he had already been cautioned earlier in the match. It was his third dismissal in the space of 27 Premiership matches, although the general consensus was that it was more a case of bad timing than malicious intent.

Even so, the punishment was a one-match suspension, which meant Townsend missed a 1-0 setback at the hands of Chelsea, the team's first home defeat of the season. He then sat out another three games after suffering a foot injury in a 4-1 victory at West Ham, but if his timing had been poor against Forest, it was perfect as he returned for the fourth round League Cup tie against QPR.

It was a match which evoked memories for Little of his playing days. During the build-up he was reminded by the media of his exploits against Rangers in the semi-final of the same competition 18 years earlier, when he had netted a hat-trick in a replay at Highbury after the teams had finished all square at Loftus Road and Villa Park. Better still, he had gone on to score twice as Villa beat Everton 3-2 in the second replay of the final at Old Trafford, following stalemates at Wembley and Hillsborough. "I'm not one for dwelling on the past," he said. "But it would be a great feeling to go to a Wembley cup final as a manager."

Little also admitted it was a bonus to have Townsend available again, particularly with Ian Taylor ruled out by injury, and the fit-again midfielder repaid his manager's faith by scoring the only goal in a victory which wasn't totally convincing, but which meant another stride had been taken along the path to a second final in the space of three years. The deadlock against a QPR team struggling in the lower reaches of the Premiership was broken on the hour mark when Paul McGrath lofted a 40-yard pass towards the visitors' goal, Dwight Yorke chested the ball down and Townsend volleyed into the far corner.

His other goal that season was the winner in a 3-2 home success over Sheffield Wednesday in early March, an explosive cross-shot worthy of winning any game. But his real moment of glory lay in wait at Wembley later in the month.

Following his single, crucial strike against QPR, Villa had reached the League Cup final by edging out neighbours Wolverhampton Wanderers 1-0 in the quarter-final and then beating Arsenal on away goals in the semi-final after their two-legged tie against the Gunners finished level at 2-2. The club, the competition's inaugural winners in 1961, had clinched a place in the final for the seventh time – and they produced a majestic performance to lift the trophy for the fifth time. Two years after he had followed Kevin Richardson up the 39 steps to the Royal Box, this time it was Townsend who led the way and collected the trophy before proudly showing it to Villa's ecstatic fans. He had been a leader on the pitch, too, turning in a perpetual motion performance which earned him the Man of the Match award as his team brushed aside Leeds United 3-0 in one of the most one-sided finals in League Cup history.

"That was a far different kettle of fish to the final against United two years earlier," says Andy. "Brian Little had put together a really good team for Villa. We had youth, we had pace and we had great ability. Everyone knew how special Dwight Yorke could be and with Savo Milosevic, you were always waiting for something to happen. Maybe he hadn't done it on a regular basis but in training he would suddenly do something that made you go 'wow!' We also had good energy in the middle of the park, and in Gareth Southgate, Paul McGrath and Ugo Ehiogu we had a great back line. Then there was Bozzie, who was an outstanding goalkeeper.

"So we felt very confident going into that final, while Leeds were far different from the side who had won the title five years earlier. Their team was effectively on its last legs. We dominated the game and they hardly threatened us.

"Once again, it was brilliant when the final whistle went. Funnily enough, I hadn't really thought about the fact I was captain this time and that I would be the one collecting the trophy if we won. But when it happened, it was pretty special and I would say that was the most satisfying moment of my career. Playing in the World Cup finals was obviously memorable and I was proud to represent my country. But as an individual, receiving a major trophy on behalf of your team takes some beating. Someone has to lift the cup, and when it's you doing it, it's a very satisfying moment, there's no denying that."

Villa's Wembley triumph ensured them of a place in the following season's UEFA Cup competition. A subsequent first-round pairing against the Swedish part-timers Helsingborg, suggested they faced a comfortable passage to the next stage.

The experienced Townsend wasn't so sure. Although he had played against Helsingborg for Chelsea in a friendly six years earlier, he admitted he knew little about them. All the same, he insisted, Villa would show the part-timers a healthy respect. "Being in Europe says your team are doing okay," he said at the time. "But there's not a lot of satisfaction in just being there. You have to do well."

In the event, Townsend and his pals possibly paid their Scandinavian opponents a little too much respect. After a 1-1 home draw, the teams drew 0-0 in the second leg, which sent the underdogs through on the away goals rule. In between times, at least the skipper had the pleasure of scoring one of the most inventive goals of the Premiership era, a classic execution from a novel free-kick against his former team Chelsea at Stamford Bridge.

With Townsend, Dwight Yorke and Serbian midfielder Sasa Curcic lined up on the edge of the penalty area, it looked for all the world as if one of them would touch the ball back for Mark Draper to try a shot. But when Yorke touched it sideways, Townsend peeled away from the three-man line and unleashed a powerful, curling left-foot drive which flew past goalkeeper Kevin Hitchcock and into the top corner. It sent visiting fans into raptures and even brought grudging applause from some Chelsea supporters, even if Townsend later admitted his superb goal had come as something of a surprise to him. "We've worked a lot of the move in training," he revealed, "but that's the first time the ball's gone in the net. The rest are in a field somewhere!"

That comment epitomised the self-effacing Townsend but there was no doubt about his importance to the team. He again scored against one of his old clubs as Villa beat Southampton 1-0 at The Dell to climb to fourth place early in December, and began to attract attention from north of the border, manager Little turning down a tempting £800,000 offer from Celtic to make sure his captain remained in claret and blue.

Ironically, a Villa player did take the high road to Parkhead the following summer, although it wasn't Townsend. While striker Tommy Johnson joined Celtic for £2.5m, the out-of-contract skipper signed a one-year deal, with the option of renewing it for a further 12 months. Ideally, he would have preferred the security of a two-year extension to his contract but his boss assured him he still had an important role to play at Villa Park. "We want to keep the nucleus of the squad together and Andy has consistently been one of our most important players," said Little. "We're delighted that he's staying."

No doubt the Villa boss meant every word but in the light of what transpired, his statement appears to have a hollow ring to it. Far from earning the opportunity to take up his second-year option, Townsend barely started his first. Three weeks into the new season, he was sold to Middlesbrough for £600,000.

On reflection, he must have wished he had left at the end of 1996-97 and gone out on a high, having helped the club to an admirable fifth place in the table. Instead, his departure came on the back of Villa's worst-ever start to a league campaign. Townsend played in the first two matches, a 1-0 defeat at Leicester City and a nightmare 4-0 home thrashing by Blackburn Rovers, before missing the 1-0 reverse at Newcastle because of an injury he had sustained playing for the Republic of Ireland. He was back in midfield for the 3-2 midweek defeat at Tottenham Hotspur, but within 48 hours his time as a Villa player was at an end.

As his team-mates prepared for the next day's match at home to Leeds United (a fixture which would yield their first win of the new campaign) and contemplated a first round UEFA Cup tie with French club Girondins de Bordeaux, he was heading to Teesside to link up with Bryan Robson at The Riverside, where he helped Boro to promotion back to the Premiership after a one-season absence.

The move came as a complete surprise, even to the player himself, although Little insisted the decision to sell had been made "in the best interests of the team."

"Andy has been fantastic for us," said the manager. "But we have made definite decisions in the last week about where we are and where we want to be. In the long term, this could give a place to Sasa Curcic; in the even longer term, we will be looking at Lee Hendrie."

What Little was saying, effectively, was that an offer of £600,000 from Middlesbrough was too good to turn down for a 34-year-old he would have to start thinking of replacing sooner rather than later. At the time it seemed a logical piece of thinking. In hindsight, Little must have wished he had persevered with the experienced Townsend for at least the remainder of the season.

Curcic, at the time Villa's £4m record signing, came briefly into the reckoning after the Ireland international's departure, despite having walked out of training following a massive row earlier that week. But it became increasingly clear that the surly Serbian midfielder had no future at Villa Park and he was offloaded to Crystal Palace for just £1m the following March. By then, Little had also gone, having resigned a month earlier and been replaced by John Gregory.

The team's fortunes improved dramatically following Gregory's appointment and from potential relegation candidates when he took over in February, they ended up qualifying for the following season's UEFA Cup. But it's tempting to suggest that they wouldn't have slipped so close to the danger zone if Andy Townsend had remained in claret and blue. He certainly thinks so.

"I shouldn't have left when I did," he says. "Brian had been willing to give me an extra two years on my contract but Doug Ellis insisted that I should only have one, which is crazy when you think I played for three more seasons in the Premiership. I felt I should have been with Villa for another season, at least. As captain, I always played my part in making the dressing room environment a happy one and a fun one. It was one where we all had a laugh but where, come Saturday, it meant a lot to us to win.

"I've always felt that the team who won the League Cup in 1996 broke up much too quickly. For the first time since Ron Atkinson's team had gone close to winning the title, we had a core of players capable of finishing in the top three. Yet within a couple of years of the final against Leeds, six or seven of us had gone. That was a great pity."

ANDY TOWNSEND - CAREER STATS

BORN:	Maidstone
DATE OF BIRTH:	July 23 1963
JOINED VILLA:	July 1993
VILLA LEAGUE APPS:	134
GOALS:	8
VILLA CUP APPS:	42
GOALS:	3
INT. CAPS (Rep of Ireland):	70
GOALS:	7

Leeds United's Eric Cantona is on the end of a Paul McGrath
challenge in a 1-1 draw at Elland Road, September 1992

Again it's Leeds United who are denied by McGrath, as
Rod Wallace is stopped in his tracks at Villa Park

McGrath just fails to foil Uwe Rosler's shot in time
at Villa Park against Manchester City, May 1995

Gareth Southgate congratulates goalscorer McGrath after the veteran had opened the scoring with a rare goal against Tottenham Hotspur, January 1996

The Villa faithful offer their salute to a true Villa legend

Despite being surrounded by Nottingham Forest players, Dwight Yorke manages to give Villa the lead at the City Ground, December 1995

Yorke celebrates after sealing matters with the third goal in the 1996 League Cup final against Leeds United at Wembley

Dwight just fails to connect with this overhead kick against Tottenham at Villa Park

Mark Bosnich sees the funny side as he and Dwight walk off

Bozzie finds himself the centre of attention against Athletic Bilbao
during the UEFA Cup second round, first-leg tie, October 1997

Dean Saunders fires home his second goal and Aston Villa's third on
his home debut against former club Liverpool, September 1992

Deano seals the 1994 League Cup final from the spot - his second
goal - as Villa stun favourites Manchester United 3-1

Andy Townsend challenges Republic of Ireland team-mate Roy Keane during the 1994 League Cup final and (below), lifting the trophy as skipper two years later

The skipper opens the scoring against Nottingham Forest, September 1995 while (below) Ian Taylor smashes home the winner against Liverpool the following season

Celebrations for Ian Taylor after scoring at Ipswich Town (top) and West Ham

Taylor challenging Chelsea's Frank Leboeuf during the 2000 FA Cup final

Goalscorers Dwight Yorke, Savo Milosevic and Ian
Taylor celebrate after the 1996 League Cup final

Gareth Southgate earns the plaudits of George Boateng after scoring the winner
against Southampton in the FA Cup fourth round, January 2000

The Villa skipper makes his voice heard

Paul Merson shows off his new colours after signing from Middlesbrough in 1998

Merse is helped off the pitch by physio Jim Walker after colliding with Leeds' Michael Duberry during the dramatic FA Cup fifth-round victory over United, January 2000

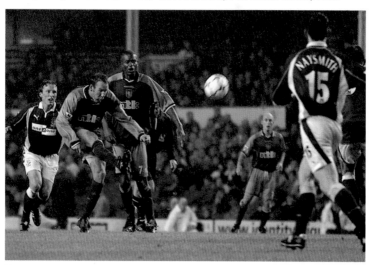

This long-range last-minute stunner from Merse hands Villa three points against Everton at Goodison Park, November 2000

Lee Hendrie and Dion Dublin celebrate the latter's winner against Middlesbrough, while (below) Dion seals Villa's place in the 2000 FA Cup final with the winning spot-kick

Joy for Dion (who headed the first) after Lee Hendrie had put Villa back on track to a rare win at Liverpool in 2001, and (below) Gareth Barry celebrates a goal at Sunderland

Skipper Barry applauds the Villa fans at the end of the game having earned his team a point with a late equaliser in the 1-1 draw with Tottenham Hotspur, October 2006

Ian Taylor

"Get lost!"

Ian Taylor's initial response was as biting as one of his tackles. And his wide-eyed smile suggested he didn't believe a word I had said.

His follow-up comment was delivered in a softer tone, albeit with equal incredulity. "You *are* joking?" he asked.

No, I wasn't joking. I wouldn't have joked in those circumstances. We were sheltering from the rain outside Sutton Coldfield Crematorium following the funeral of Stan Arthurs, a lifelong Villa supporter well known for his regular Friday lunchtime visits to Bodymoor Heath.

Stan, who had died a week earlier at the age of 84, would have been delighted that Tayls had taken the trouble to turn up and pay his last respects, despite having left the club almost four years earlier.

The old fellow would also have approved of the news I had just imparted – that Ian Taylor had been voted one of Villa's top 10 Premiership players.

Typical of his modest, unassuming nature, Ian couldn't quite get his head around his inclusion, particularly when I mentioned a few of those who had missed the cut, outstanding players like Steve Staunton, Olof Mellberg, Kevin Richardson and Ugo Ehiogu.

Then again, it was no great surprise that he should be taken aback. Throughout his career, he was never a player who went looking for accolades, being content to go about his business in an understated manner which rarely propelled him into the spotlight, but which made him invaluable to his team-mates. The phrase players' player could have been invented just for him.

He was always reluctant to face the media, too. I wouldn't like to hazard a guess at the number of times he greeted requests for an interview with the words, delivered in mock annoyance: "What do *you* want?" Eventually, though, he would oblige with answers which were never going to make sensational headlines, but invariably made a lot of sense.

If he was a footballer of few words, his facial expressions, sometimes happy, occasionally sad, usually told exactly what he was thinking. That was never more evident than when Alan Shearer was sent off against Villa at St. James' Park on the opening day of the 1999-2000 season. The Newcastle striker's dismissal was for two bookable offences but the second, when he backed into Villa defender Colin Calderwood, looked innocuous in the extreme.

Referee Uriah Rennie's decision to caution the England star surprised almost everyone in the ground, not least Magpies manager Ruud Gullit, who publicly admonished the Sheffield official afterwards. But the enduring image of the controversial incident was a TV shot of Taylor, who was standing behind Shearer as the red card was brandished. His disbelief was there for all to see as he was captured with his eyebrows raised and his hand to his mouth to prevent himself from laughing out loud.

There had been no need for Ian Taylor to try to suppress his feelings four years and eight months earlier, when his face had revealed everything about how he was feeling. It was a couple of days before Christmas in 1994 and he was standing proudly on the pitch at Villa Park with a beaming smile on his face and Brian Little's hand on his shoulder. He had just become the new manager's first signing, arriving from Sheffield Wednesday in an exchange deal which saw striker Guy Whittingham move to Hillsborough.

It was a transfer which attracted little attention outside the West Midlands and South Yorkshire, but it meant everything to Ian Taylor. At the age of 26, he had fulfilled his long-time ambition of joining the club he had supported as a boy. "I really can't believe it," he told the assembled gathering of reporters and photographers. "This is a dream come true for me."

His delight was perfectly understandable. After all, he had frequently cheered on his heroes from the Holte End and had cheered them to victory over Barcelona in the European Super Cup early in 1983.

Ideally, he would have been snapped up by Villa as a youngster and progressed through the ranks, just like Villa fans Luke Moore, Gabby Agbonlahor and Craig Gardner have in more recent times. As it was, there had seemed little prospect of him becoming a professional footballer during his childhood years in Stetchford, deep in Birmingham City territory. In that area, it was hard enough just being a Villa supporter, although Ian was far from alone in his devotion to claret and blue.

"My mate across the road was also a Villa fan," he says. "We went together from the age of nine or 10. We used to get in for nothing when they opened the turnstiles in the second half! I can't remember my first match, but we always stood on the Holte End. I didn't really have any stick at school because there were plenty of Villa fans there, even though it was a Blues area.

"I even played for the Washwood Heath School team in the Aston Villa Cup final at Villa Park when I was 12. I still have a photo and me and my mate – and I'm wearing my little Villa sweat band. We beat Archbishop Grimshaw and it was a nice feeling to win at Villa Park.

"But I never seriously thought about being a professional. When I left school I went on an electricians' course, but don't ask me to come and do any electrical work for you. I didn't have much idea, I'm afraid. But I needed to earn some money so I got a job as a forklift truck driver for SEP Fasteners in Dudley at £90-a-week.

"It didn't bother me too much that I hadn't been taken on by any of the local clubs. To be honest, I never thought I was good enough – certainly not as good as some of the lads I'd played alongside at school. It wasn't the be-all-and-end-all for me. When Bob Faulkner signed me for Moor Green, I was happy playing for them on a Saturday and watching Villa whenever I could in midweek."

Ian's time in non-League football turned out to be more productive than he could ever have imagined. He started attracting attention from several League clubs and finally made it as a pro at the age of 24 when he was signed by Port Vale for the princely sum of £15,000. In two highly-successful seasons in the Potteries, he averaged a goal every three games, helping Vale to two Wembley finals in 1993, savouring victory over Stockport County in the Autoglass Trophy but missing out to West Bromwich Albion in the Second Division play-off final.

While he loved every minute of his time in Burslem, the call of the Premiership was too strong to resist and in the summer of 1994 he joined Sheffield Wednesday in a £1m deal. Unfortunately, things didn't turn out quite as he expected at Hillsborough, where he made numerous appearances but was frequently played out of position by manager Trevor Francis and felt far from settled. But by the end of the year, he was on his way back to the Midlands. Wednesday were looking to sign a striker while Villa wanted to strengthen their midfield, so Whittingham headed to Hillsborough while Taylor finally joined the club he loved.

"My agent told me Villa were interested and asked if I wanted to go there," he recalls. "I said: 'Damn right I do!' Then Trevor called me into his office and said: 'You'll never believe who's come in for you.' I was struggling to keep the smile off my face because I already knew, but I just said: 'No, who?' He said: 'It's your team, Villa. Do you want to go?' I said: 'Do I?!!!' I certainly didn't need asking twice. And that was it – I was off to Villa. It was great going back home again, too, because I'd moved up to Sheffield and was travelling back every weekend."

While he was bursting with pride as he posed for pictures following his signing, there was no time to dwell on his delight at becoming an Aston Villa player. Little had not bought him to fulfil his dream, he had done so because he had identified Taylor as a player capable of helping to keep Villa in the top flight. A 2-1 defeat at Southampton the previous Monday had left them struggling just two places off the bottom of the table, and there was a difficult match at Arsenal coming up on Boxing Day. A great deal of work was needed to lift Villa out of the relegation zone, and Little had earmarked his new boy for a sizeable share of it.

"He's a player who can play from box-to-box and really covers the ground," said the manager. "He scores goals, which is a tremendous asset for a midfield player, and we will be encouraging him to get into goalscoring positions."

There was little prospect of a Taylor debut goal at Highbury, particularly after skipper Andy Townsend had been sent off just past the hour mark, but the 0-0 draw in north London was followed a couple of nights later by a spectacle which embraced the feel-good factor of the pantomime season.

It was the night the upper tier of the all-seater Holte End was opened for the first time, and while it hardly resembled the terrace from which Taylor had once watched his favourites, he certainly wasn't complaining as he met Dwight Yorke's centre with a firm header which completed an emphatic 3-0 victory, the team's first at home in the league since early September – and Taylor had actually played a small part in denying Little a winning start during that depressing sequence. A month before his Villa home debut, he had gone on as an 82nd-minute substitute for Sheffield Wednesday at Villa Park as the Owls forced a 1-1 draw in the new manager's first match in charge.

"I have to say I can't remember much about that, or of Andy getting sent off at Highbury on my debut," he says. "But I certainly remember that game against Chelsea. Scoring in front of the Holte End on my home debut was an incredible feeling. It was all the more special because all my family and friends were there. Brilliant!"

Even though the remainder of the season proved to be a war of attrition for Little's men, there was never any question about Tayls being far from the heat of the battle. True, he was kicking himself after squandering a glorious late chance in a 2-2 draw at Manchester City on New Year's Eve, but his dynamic displays became the norm as he continued popping up in both penalty areas, winning possession in midfield and using the ball constructively. The latter quality was perfectly illustrated on his return to Hillsborough, where he was close to scoring on a couple of occasions as well as providing the low, angled cross from which Dean Saunders netted the first of his two goals in a 2-1 win. If Francis wasn't already regretting his decision to let the industrious midfielder join Villa, he surely did so that afternoon.

Tayls was, without doubt, making massive strides. Initially content to play safe by making short, first-time passes, he began to hold the ball longer as his confidence grew and showed a willingness to run with it from his own half. He was rapidly becoming, as Andy Colquhoun observed in the *Birmingham Post*, "the heart of Little's Villa."

That heart skipped a few beats, Taylor readily acknowledges, before Villa assured themselves of continued tenancy in the top flight with a draw at Norwich City on the final day. He missed that game through injury, but admits: "It was a massive relief when we stayed up. For me, it was great to be playing regularly for Villa but I wouldn't have fancied the idea that I'd signed in December and they had been relegated in May. That would have been terrible, both for me and for the club. Playing for Villa was always something special, it never became just a job, but it helped that I played all my football for the club at the top level."

Having experienced a few flutters during the club's flirtation with relegation, Taylor subsequently became a major influence in a highly successful team. The following season was just 14 minutes old when he applied the finishing touch to a low cross from Gary Charles and set in motion a famous 3-1 victory over Manchester United. His mobility was an important factor, too, throughout a campaign in which Villa finished fourth in the league, reached the FA Cup semi-finals and lifted the League Cup for the second time in three seasons.

If Wembley Stadium on Sunday 24th March was a special place for everyone connected with the club, it was particularly so for Ian Taylor, who found himself acting out a third fantasy in the space of 15 months. Joining Villa and scoring on his home debut had been the stuff of dreams; scoring for his favourite team in a Wembley final was something else again. It was the goal which effectively secured the trophy, too. Savo Milosevic had opened the scoring with a magnificent 25-yard drive in the 20th minute and from that juncture there was never any real question about the outcome. While the score remained 1-0, though, an outclassed Leeds United side were still in contention and Villa were aware of the need for a second goal to extinguish their opponents' hopes of a fightback. It arrived nine minutes into the second half when Alan Wright's centre was hooked away by Lucas Radebe but only as far as Taylor, who unleashed a stunning left-foot volley past goalkeeper John Lukic.

"It was brilliant to win something so soon after joining Villa," he says. "I'd only been at the club for just over 15 months when we beat Leeds at Wembley but there had been a massive turnaround of players during that time. We improved so quickly.

"I was pretty lucky, really. I'd played twice for Port Vale at Wembley and now I was back there with Villa. I'd been as a spectator when they beat Manchester United in the final two years earlier. I went on a supporters' coach with my mates. So scoring at the end where I'd been sitting in 1994 was just amazing. When the ball went in, I ran over to Tommy Johnson, who was a sub that day and had been running up the touchline. It was great to think I'd scored in front of all the Villa fans – and I still have a picture of my name up in lights on the Wembley scoreboard. When I had joined Villa, I could never have imagined that happening. It was great just to be playing for the club at Wembley but to score; well…

"It was such a magical place and I don't think the new stadium will ever have the same feel to it. I went to the Derby v West Brom play-off match and to be honest I don't think the new one is a patch on the old stadium. They've even taken away that long walk from the tunnel end, where players could take in the whole atmosphere as they walked from the dressing rooms to the middle of the pitch."

Hardly surprisingly, Ian regards scoring in that final as the highlight of his career, although has equal affection for the goal he scored at the Holte End on his home debut. They were, quite simply, two moments which no amount of money could buy.

By the end of that season, he had further underlined his value to the club, helping out in defence when Steve Staunton was injured. It was no great surprise, then, when he was rewarded that summer with a new four-year contract. "His versatility makes him very important," said Little at the time. "He complements Andy Townsend and Mark Draper in midfield, but when I had to play him in defence at the end of last season, he was outstanding."

It would be some time before his defensive qualities were required again, but that in no way diminished his input. The arrival of Serb Sasa Curcic from Bolton Wanderers fleetingly put his place under threat and he was on the substitutes' bench for a spell during the early weeks of the following season. But it soon became apparent that Villa operated more effectively with the local lad than with the man who had cost a club record £4m.

Essentially, there was only one thing lacking from his game, and it was the regular supply of goals which Little had predicted on the day he signed. After two-and-a-half seasons in claret and blue, his haul amounted to a very modest nine, although one of them, in March 1997, could hardly have been more important. His late winner against Liverpool at Villa Park, fired clinically past David James after he had controlled Townsend's cross with his knee, was Villa's first against the Merseysiders in more than 580 minutes of football. Previously, we had endured a depressing run of four straight defeats at the hands of the Anfield outfit, conceding 11 and failing to provide a single reply. No wonder Taylor's strike was so rapturously applauded by the capacity crowd.

Having seen off the challenge presented by Curcic, who would eventually be sold to Crystal Palace for just a quarter of what he had cost, Ian's place was again briefly under threat at the start of the 1997-98 campaign. Although he played in the 1-0 opening-day defeat at Leicester, Little left him out for the following Wednesday's home match against Blackburn Rovers in an attempt to accommodate Dwight Yorke, Savo Milosevic and £7m record signing Stan Collymore in the same line-up. Half-an-hour into the game, with Villa being outfought and outplayed, not to mention being two-down, supporters started calling for his introduction from the subs' bench. At half-time, Little heeded the demands of the fans, sending him on in place of Ugo Ehiogu, although by that time Chris Sutton had completed a hat-trick for the visitors.

Blackburn went on to win 4-0 although the second half was far more competitive, and while Taylor was unable to prevent a dreadful run of four consecutive defeats – the worst start in the club's history – his omission from the starting line-up against Rovers was a mistake his manager was in no hurry to repeat.

Tayls started 42 league and cup games that season, his highest figure to date, and the goals started flowing, too. He doubled his Villa output with nine in as many months, and a third of them came on European nights at Villa Park. Nearly 15 years earlier, he had savoured the special atmosphere of that European Super Cup triumph over Barcelona from the terraces. Now he was occupying centre stage against some of the continent's finest teams. Savo Milosevic was the single-goal hero against Girondins de Bordeaux in the opening round, the Serb striker clinching a 1-0 aggregate win in extra time at Villa Park – but then Tayls took over.

After another goalless away leg in the second round against Athletic Bilbao, the return match was balanced on a knife-edge for almost half-an-hour before Villa made a crucial breakthrough. Accepting a pass from Steve Staunton, Milosevic turned away from his marker before delivering a left-wing centre which, in fairness, goalkeeper Imanol Etxeberria should really have held. But the keeper, possibly distracted by Dwight Yorke's close attendance, allowed the ball to slip from his grasp, allowing Taylor to sidefoot into the net from six yards.

The industrious midfielder also set up the second goal for Yorke early in the second half as Villa went through 2-1, and he then secured victory over Steaua Bucharest in the third round. Having lost 2-1 in Romania, Villa knew a 1-0 verdict on home soil would be sufficient to see them through on the away goals rule. Milosevic duly provided it on 71 minutes but Villa then faced a nail-biting finale in the knowledge that a Steaua equaliser would knock them out. Tayls, thankfully, had other ideas, calmly slotting home his team's second goal four minutes from time to see Villa through to the last eight of the UEFA Cup for the first time in 20 years.

By the time the quarter-final against Atletico Madrid rolled around the following spring, John Gregory had succeeded Little as manager. Not that a change of boss made any difference to Ian Taylor, who simply wouldn't have been capable of giving less than 100 per cent, regardless of who was in charge. In the event, there was nothing Tayls, or any of his colleagues could do to prevent the men from Madrid going through to the semi-finals. Christian Vieri's penalty, awarded when Taylor was adjudged to have brought down Jose Luis Caminero, was all that separated the teams in the first leg at the Vicente Calderon Stadium, but Villa were left facing an almighty battle when Caminero put the visitors ahead after 28 minutes at Villa Park two weeks later. That left Gregory's boys needing to score three times against one of the most organised sides in Europe and while they failed to do so, it was a glorious failure.

With 18 minutes remaining, Atletico's two-goal advantage was still intact and most of the near-capacity crowd held out little hope of a comeback. Yet it very nearly materialised, Taylor equalising with a shot which deflected off substitute Daniel Prodan before Stan Collymore's unstoppable drive two minutes later which almost lifted the roof off both the net and the Holte End stand. Unfortunately, the Spanish giants survived the final 16 minutes with no further damage to their battered ego. Atletico, beaten 2-1 on the night, were through on away goals; Villa, having secured a glorious victory in front of their own supporters, were out.

"All of the European nights were great", says Taylor, "but the game against Atletico was electrifying. When Stan hit that shot into the top corner, the roar was unbelievable. I know we went out, but for atmosphere, that was the best I ever experienced at Villa Park. If we had scored again and gone through, I can't even begin to imagine what it would have been like."

Despite suffering injuries at various stages of the following campaign, Taylor was still an integral member of a side who enjoyed the best start in the club's history before slipping back to sixth in the final table. For the most part, he made his usual impact and his only real disappointment was the fact that his goals dried up again. After hitting the target nine times the previous season, he had set his heart on reaching double figures and it looked perfectly achievable when he scored in a 2-0 home win over Wimbledon and netted both goals in a 2-1 win at Coventry City in early October.

That was the first time he had scored twice in one game for Villa, but it was April before he netted again, this time claiming the only goal against Liverpool at Anfield. It was the 10th anniversary of the Hillsborough disaster that day and Villa's players and supporters duly paid their respects before the match, the fans impeccably observing a minute's silence while Mark Bosnich and Paul Merson laid floral tributes in front of the Kop.

However, once the action was under way, Villa's minds were concentrated very much on the present. No-one was more focused on the task in hand than Taylor, who steered home the winner from just three yards after Julian Joachim had miscued Alan Wright's deep centre.

While his fourth goal of the season proved to be his last, he returned to a more prolific output in 1999-00, scoring nine goals – all of them by the second week of the new Millennium. During one midwinter flurry, in fact, he was on target in four consecutive games, although one effort was subsequently declared void when the Football League ordered that the Worthington Cup quarter-final at West Ham should be re-staged after it was discovered the Hammers had fielded an ineligible player. Far from sulking over a goal which was expunged from the record books, he replaced it with two as Villa won 3-1 when the tie was re-run four weeks later – and scored yet again in a 1-1 Premiership draw at Upton Park three days later.

If his scoring was on the increase, unfortunately, so too was his penchant for falling foul of referees. Such was his total commitment to the cause, he was booked a dozen times by the night of the re-staged West Ham cup-tie, one of his cautions having been issued in the original game. It was just his luck that while the result and his goal had been declared void, the FA decided that his booking should stand. Not that he had any intention of being thrown out of his stride by the continual stream of yellow cards. "These things happen and I don't really worry about it," he said. "I wouldn't be playing my normal game if I eased off. I can't afford to think about being booked. If I did, I wouldn't be doing my job."

As it happened, it wasn't suspension which curtailed the remainder of his season, it was injury. First he was laid low by ankle damage sustained in the Worthington Cup semi-final against Leicester City, and then he tore a hamstring just 15 minutes into the FA Cup semi-final against Bolton Wanderers at Wembley. It speaks volumes for the regard in which he was held by his manager, though, that his next starting appearance was also at Wembley, when Villa faced Chelsea in the FA Cup Final. His return wasn't enough to prevent a 1-0 defeat and he was replaced by Steve Stone 11 minutes from time, but another vintage season was rewarded with a new contract.

"After I was carried off in the semi-final, I thought I had no chance of being fit for the final," he recalls. "And even if I got fit, it was on my mind that I might not play against Chelsea. But John Gregory showed faith in me and put me in from the start. I must admit that came as a surprise. It was just a shame we didn't perform on the day. It was one of those days when nothing seemed to work and it was one of my biggest disappointments as a player.

"The other thing which bugs me is not being on the photo of the lads celebrating when David James made the save which meant we had won the penalty shoot-out against Bolton. That's one of my biggest regrets. You see that photo all the time – and

I'm not on it!"

Although armed with a new deal which offered medium-term security, Tayls made a far from happy start to the first full campaign of the new century. Sent off for two bookings in a farcical Intertoto Cup tie against Celta Vigo at The Hawthorns, Ian had to settle for a seat on the bench in four of the first five league games. Once re-established in the starting line-up, however, he proved to be a man for all weather, heading the opening goal in a 2-1 win over Charlton Athletic in a Villa Park deluge and then netting twice as Tottenham Hotspur were beaten 2-0 in rather better conditions a couple of weeks later.

He also hit the winner against Everton in April, but in between times there was once again the frustration of another hamstring problem. The emergence of Lee Hendrie didn't help, either and although he finished strongly, the season ended as it had begun – with a red card.

Where he had suppressed laughter at Alan Shearer's dismissal at St. James' Park the previous season, this time he stared in disbelief when he was the one on the receiving end of a piece of harsh justice. Both he and Newcastle's Gary Speed were sent off by referee Barry Knight after a brief altercation more suited to handbags rather than boxing gloves.

"All I was doing was shielding the ball and Gary clattered into me," he insisted afterwards. "We had a bit of a scuffle but there was nothing to it really and I just can't understand why we were sent off. There was no animosity between us and Gary didn't even realise I'd been sent off."

Thankfully, the red card was rescinded, removing the threat of a three-match suspension at the start of the following season. Unfortunately, as it turned out, Taylor was missing for considerably longer. He had been carrying a knee injury and it became evident when he reported back for pre-season training that his summer rest had not cured the problem. Surgery was prescribed and it was mid-October before he was able to play in a competitive match, marking his return to action with a well-taken goal against Fulham after going on as a substitute for Moroccan midfielder Hassan Kachloul.

We all expected that to be the start of an extended run. Instead, it was merely the beginning of the end of his time at Villa Park. Twice more that season he was laid low by injuries – first his groin, then his knee – and each time he made a goalscoring return, at Sunderland on New Year's Day and at Bolton on Easter Saturday.

Graham Taylor had replaced John Gregory as manager by then and the new boss readily acknowledged just how effective a fully-fit Ian Taylor could be, handing him a one-year contract extension. But time was running out and although he scored against French club Lille in the Intertoto Cup, it was late October before he saw his first Premiership action. Typically, his return coincided with a hard-earned draw against Manchester United at Old Trafford, which launched a six-match unbeaten run for Villa. But a series of injuries, including thigh and hamstring problems, were starting to take their toll on the legs of a 34-year-old finding it increasingly difficult to function in the engine room of a Premiership team.

On the eve of the final match of the 2002-2003 season against Leeds United, he was told he would play some part at Elland Road, but that he was not being offered a new contract.

"It was a damp squib really," he says. "In a way, I could see it coming because I was struggling with injuries at the time and I was getting on a bit. But I was close to tears when Graham told me. I just wish he'd said something before our last home match against Sunderland the week before. Then I could have had a proper send-off and said goodbye to the fans. Instead, no-one knew I'd been released until after the Leeds match."

In an ideal world, Ian Taylor would have seen out his playing career at Villa Park, proudly wearing the colours of his boyhood favourites until his legs gave out on him. In the event, his playing days were arguably extended because he left. Two years with Derby County were followed by another two at Northampton Town before he finally hung up his boots in April 2007, just over a month short of his 39th birthday. It's hard to envisage that he would have continued so long in the Premiership.

If he was no longer around Villa Park, though, he was most certainly not forgotten by the legions of fans who had idolised him for so long. During his time as a Villa player he had regularly been spotted among travelling supporters at away matches whenever he was injured, prompting a chorus of "There's only one Ian Taylor." He continued to attend games during his time with the Rams and the Cobblers, too, and now he is no longer playing, his presence among the claret and blue army is set to increase considerably.

Such is the esteem in which he is held that several hundred Villa supporters also attended his farewell match for Northampton on a Friday night before reminding the world at the City of Manchester Stadium the following afternoon that there's only one Ian Taylor.

Strictly speaking they are wrong because it's not an uncommon name. But in the eyes of Villa folk this Ian Taylor, as ordinary as his name, is in many ways a legend. With the exception of Paul McGrath, it's hard to think of another player who could command such a following on a Friday night in Northampton, four years after leaving Villa.

"It wasn't quite the same as it would have been at Villa Park," he says. "But it was fantastic that so many of them came over to the game. It had been arranged beforehand that I would play for an hour and then come off, which is what happened. The crowd gave me a great reception as I left the pitch – and then I noticed that most of the Villa fans were leaving the ground!"

Having paid tribute to one of their own, the Villa contingent had no further interest in Northampton's 1-1 draw against

Huddersfield Town and had clearly decided to head for the nearest pub. If Ian Taylor had known where they were drinking, he would probably have joined them for a pint.

IAN TAYLOR - CAREER STATS	
BORN:	Birmingham
DATE OF BIRTH:	June 4 1968
JOINED VILLA:	December 1994
VILLA LEAGUE APPS:	233
GOALS:	28
VILLA CUP APPS:	57
GOALS	14
INT. CAPS (England):	0
GOALS:	0

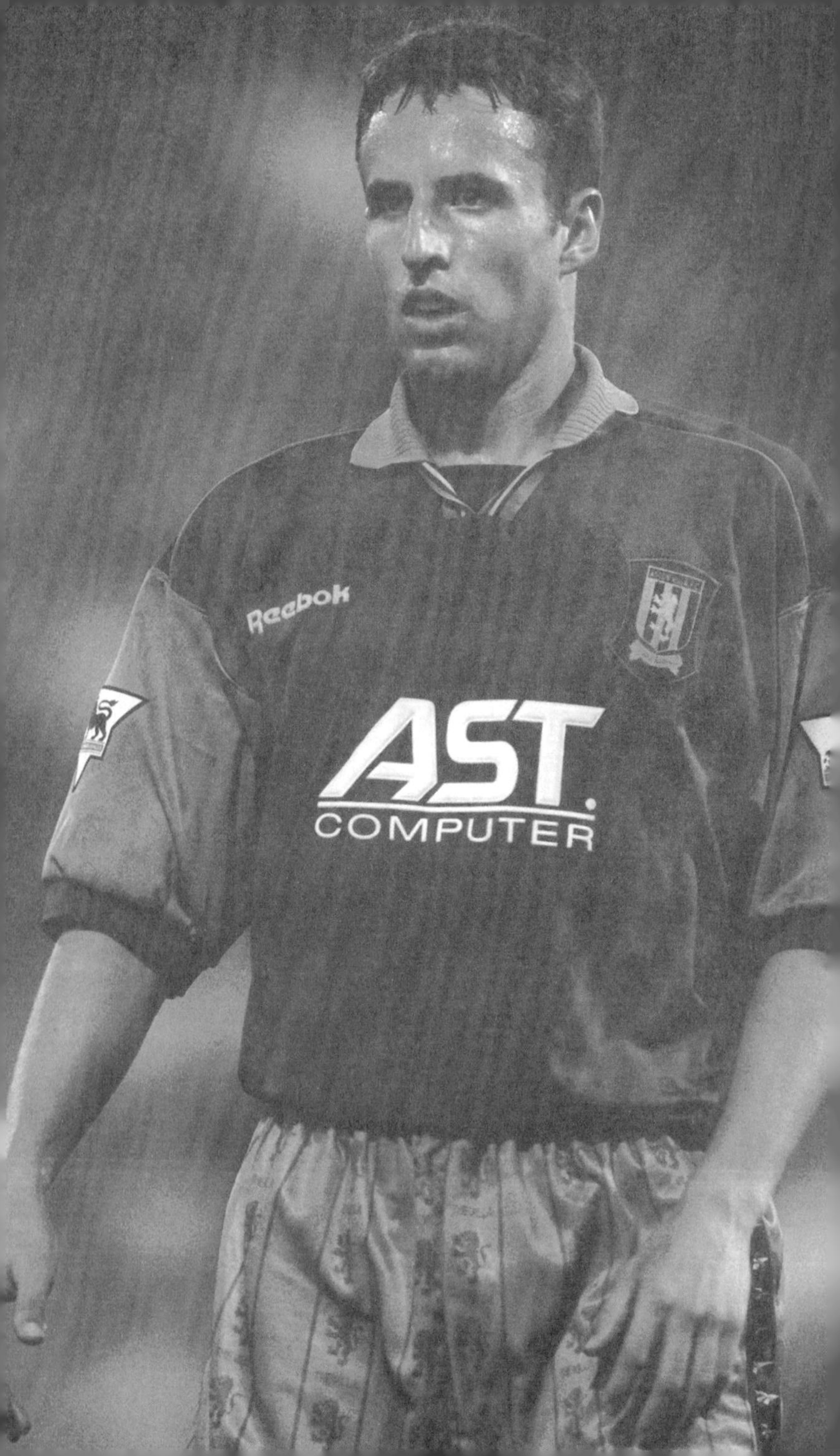
Reebok
AST
COMPUTER

1995-2001

Gareth
Southgate

The interview could hardly have been going any more smoothly when Gareth Southgate suddenly led me into temptation. One essential ground rule had been established at the outset and I'd had no intention of breaking it. Not initially, at least. Not until he presented me with the sort of opening he rarely gave to opposition forwards.

It was a few months after his infamous penalty miss which meant England's players could put their feet up while Germany prepared for the Euro '96 final against the Czech Republic.

Southgate was still coming to terms with the consequences of his weakly-struck spot-kick at Wembley and was refusing to talk about it publicly. But that didn't really matter when I contacted him on behalf of a new magazine called *Drive On*, aimed at people who had just passed their driving test. My brief didn't include penalties, or even football, for that matter. I had been asked to write an article about Gareth's first car.

I promised him beforehand that there would be no reference to Euro '96, Germans or missed penalties and he happily chatted away about a bright yellow Vauxhall Cavalier, "which I bought from my dad for a couple of quid and drove until it fell apart."

Having described the vehicle and some of his outings in it, he recalled the day he took his driving test and volunteered: "That was the most nerve-racking thing I've ever known."

Well, what would you have done? I know I'd promised otherwise but his comment begged the obvious question. Clearing my throat, I asked him nervously: "Even more nerve-racking than taking that penalty?"

Thankfully, he just chuckled and said yes, it had been. He clearly wasn't going to expand on that fateful June night at Wembley, but he was perfectly happy for the comparison to appear in print. My question subsequently appeared as a headline in the first issue of the magazine – with an exclamation mark replacing the question mark.

That said everything about Gareth Southgate, the thinking man's footballer. Articulate, intelligent and polite, he also had a sense of humour, and while there was no way he was going to reveal his inner thoughts on missing against Germany, he could also see no harm, five months after the event, in his Wembley embarrassment forming the basis of a light-hearted item in a specialist magazine.

It was just a pity, from his point of view, that 1996 could not have ended in early May, when he completed a season he could only have dreamed about in his debut campaign at Villa Park. League Cup winners, FA Cup semi-finalists, fourth in the Premiership – it was, indeed, a time for any Aston Villa man to savour.

"It was a fantastic season, right from the opening-day win against Manchester United," he recalls. "That set us up for the whole season and we had a team with great balance – a good mixture of youth and experience. We were also fortunate with injuries and it was a fairly settled team all the way through.

"The highlight was obviously the final against Leeds United. I'd reached two semi-finals with Crystal Palace the previous year, so it was great to get to my first final and even better to win. It was a good time to play Leeds because they were really struggling, but that said, I believe we would have been good value against anyone that day."

While there was never any question about Southgate's burning desire for success, he always pursued it with dignity. He played the game hard but fairly, and was the perfect gentleman off the pitch. Even after asking for a transfer just before heading off with the England squad for Euro 2000, he gave a season of outstanding service in claret and blue. He may have made it clear that he wanted to leave by that stage, but he wasn't about to short-change the club who were still paying his wages. Andy Townsend, the man he had succeeded as Villa captain, could see that.

"You know what you are going to get with Gareth," said Townsend. "That's nine out of 10 every week. He has always remained focused on the job in hand. He goes about his job in an unfussy, uncomplicated way and is massively underrated."

It had always been that way, to be fair, and many people were surprised that Brian Little should make Southgate one of his major targets in the summer of 1995. The Villa manager, though, had clearly done his homework. He had earmarked the Palace midfielder as a player with an abundance of both mobility and ability, and believed his full season as skipper of the Eagles would stand him in good stead for life at Villa Park.

The manager obviously had a good memory, too. The previous November, in only Little's second match after replacing Ron Atkinson, Villa had been on the receiving end of a 4-1 League Cup drubbing by Palace at Selhurst Park and two of the goals were scored by Southgate.

By the time he left south London, in fact, Southgate had scored 22 times for the Eagles and was generally regarded as a midfielder who was capable of playing in defence. We weren't to know that by the time he pulled on a claret and blue shirt for the first time in competitive action, his career path as a centre-back had effectively been mapped out. As temperatures soared and Villa prepared for a spending spree which would climb to more than £9m, we didn't particularly concern ourselves with what position the new signing would occupy on the opening day of the new season.

As Southgate put pen to paper on a four-year contract on Friday 23rd June 1995, the only thing on everyone's minds was that this polite, amiable young man had just become the club's £2.5m record signing, costing a couple of hundred thousand more than Dean Saunders just under three years earlier.

"I wanted to play on a big stage and this is it," said Gareth as he faced the media after completing his move to the Midlands. "When I asked for a transfer at Palace after they got relegated, the thing they said to me was to make sure I got a big club. I'm sure I have. I wasn't aware that I was the club's record signing until it was mentioned in the press conference but that doesn't concern me. I don't expect it will be a record that lasts long."

Indeed it wasn't. Even before the day was out, a new record had been established. As we stood chatting on the Villa Park pitch after Southgate had posed for the obligatory round of photographs in the late-morning sunshine, no-one took a great deal of notice as Little and chairman Doug Ellis slipped away early. Unbeknown to us, they were heading to Birmingham International Airport for a flight to Belgrade. By midnight, striker Savo Milosevic had been signed from Partizan Belgrade for £3.5m.

Within two weeks, in fact, Southgate had slipped down to third place in the list of Villa's most expensive captures when Mark Draper arrived from Leicester City in a £3.25m deal. But while both Milosevic and Draper made a sizeable impact in Villa shirts, Southgate was destined to make the biggest of the trio.

Andy Colquhoun of the *Birmingham Post* was among those to recognise that this was a footballer with an astute mind as well as skilful feet. Pointing out that the new player would have pursued a career in journalism but for his football career, Colquhoun observed: "Southgate is a natural spokesman and is clearly a Villa captain in waiting."

Even the man from the Post, though, could not have envisaged that Southgate would be playing for England in the following year's European Championship finals – and not in the position we all imagined to be his best.

The first hint that he would be starting the campaign in defence rather than in midfield came in a 1-0 friendly defeat by neighbours West Bromwich Albion at The Hawthorns, where he was tried both as a centre-back and as a sweeper and by the time the opening game rolled around, Little had established a back three of Southgate, Paul McGrath and Ugo Ehiogu, with Gary Charles and Alan Wright operating as wing-backs.

There was understandably a touch of first-day apprehension, not least because Manchester United were the visitors but by half-time it was well and truly forgotten as Villa raced into a three-goal lead, eventually winning 3-1. All three of the new boys played their part. Draper netted the second goal and Milosevic was fouled for the penalty from which Dwight Yorke scored the third, while Southgate produced a performance which provided the template for the following six years. As Henry Winter observed in the *Daily Telegraph*: "Southgate proved a revelation at the back, giving the hosts both defensive security and a creative platform."

During the next few months, while Milosevic and Draper were frequently in the spotlight because of their more forward roles, Southgate quietly evolved into one of the best centre-backs in the country. He even found time to go on a surging run towards the end of a 6-0 League Cup romp against Peterborough United, evading three tackles before firing home his team's final goal.

But it was at the heart of the defence that he truly excelled and his calm, commanding, consistent performances did not go unnoticed by England coach Terry Venables. In December, he won his first full international cap, going on as a substitute against Portugal at Wembley. It was the first of 57 appearances for the national side and his confidence soared as a result. He rendered Manchester United danger man Eric Cantona totally ineffective in a goalless draw at Old Trafford. His stylish displays on the domestic front continued throughout the winter, to the extent that when Paul McGrath was rested for a match at Bolton in February, he effortlessly switched from the right of the back three to the centre. Ugo Ehiogu was on his right at Burnden Park, with Steve Staunton to his left and the trio were so impressive in a 2-0 win that McGrath had to settle for a seat on the bench at Highbury four days later, as Villa drew 2-2 with Arsenal in the first leg of the League Cup semi-final.

The Ehiogu-Southgate-Staunton back three also served Villa well in the second leg at Villa Park, where a 0-0 stalemate meant Little's men were through to the final on the away goals rule, and a week later Southgate scored his first league goal for Villa. His well-placed header from an Andy Townsend corner clinched a 2-0 home win over Blackburn Rovers, although he probably gained more satisfaction from the way he subdued England striker Alan Shearer.

But the crowing glory of Southgate's debut campaign was still to come. An injury sustained against Queen Park Rangers ruled him out of action for three matches but he was back in the side for the emphatic 3-0 League Cup final victory against Leeds United at Wembley. While it was a day to savour for Villa's players, though, his mind was already on the next game.

"I didn't enjoy the win as much as I might have done," he admits. "Ugo Ehiogu and I had to cut short the celebrations to join the England squad, although my mum and dad probably enjoyed the night more than anyone. They had a great time with Steve Staunton's parents-in-law."

Villa's triumph over the Yorkshire outfit launched an incredible week for Southgate, albeit one which would end painfully. Three days later he made his first starting appearance for the national side in a 1-0 friendly win over Bulgaria at Wembley, and he might well have been tempted to believe that he would be back in front of the famous twin towers for the FA Cup final. Seven days after demolishing Leeds, Little's men faced Liverpool in the semi-final at Old Trafford.

They gave a good account of themselves, too, and a 3-0 defeat hardly reflects their contribution to the afternoon's proceedings, two of Liverpool's goals coming in the closing stages of a fairly even contest. For Southgate, though, it was all over by the 22nd minute.

It was almost as if Villa's fate was sealed from the moment he wrenched his knee in a block tackle on Mark Wright. He had to leave the field for strapping to be applied and as he returned to the heart of the defence, Liverpool were preparing to take the free-kick from which Robbie Fowler headed them into a 16th-minute lead. We will never know what the outcome might have been with a fully-fit Southgate in Villa's ranks but six minutes later he was forced to withdraw from the action, being replaced by Steve Staunton. As he says, his injury underlined the highs and lows a professional footballer can experience in the space of just a week.

The big question now, given his emergence as an international-class defender, was whether he would recover in time for Euro '96. Thankfully, he was able to return to the Villa line-up for the final match of the season against Everton at Goodison Park and Venables decided he was fit enough to represent his country as Skinner & Baddiel convinced the nation in song that 30 years of hurt had never stopped us dreaming.

The dream ended, sadly, because of Southgate's tame spot-kick in the semi-final against Germany, but we should not underestimate his contribution to England's bold, brave attempt at winning their first major trophy since the 1966 World Cup. He was an integral part of a defence which conceded just three goals in five matches plus extra time in both the quarter-final against Spain and the semi against the Germans.

But all of that apparently counted for nothing after the unfortunate penalty shoot-out scenario. Whatever else may have been happening in the world on Wednesday 26th June, the following morning's front pages were concerned only with a young man called Gareth Southgate, whose failure to score a penalty had cost England a place in the Euro '96 final. The furore continued for several days, too, as media men camped outside the Southgate family home in search of follow-up stories. Even his mum, Barbara, was quoted, famously asking her son: "Why didn't you just belt it?"

Gradually, though, the fuss died down and after flying off on holiday to Bali, he reported back for pre-season training at Bodymoor Heath, encouraged by a bulging postbag of letters of support. "The reaction of the public has been superb," he said at the time. "I've had a huge bag of mail which I'm still trying to reply to. Many of the letters have put things in perspective. Writers have said far worse things have happened to them or their families."

The winning goal in the opening home game against Blackburn Rovers also helped to ease the pain of letting down his country, and he attempted to draw a line under the incident by appearing in a Pizza Hut commercial which ridiculed his penalty miss. Stuart Pearce and Chris Waddle, who had missed penalties for England against West Germany in the 1990 World Cup finals, also appeared in the advert, which showed Southgate, reluctant to show his face in public, wearing a brown paper bag over his head.

For all that, it clearly affected him deeply and even a decade later, when he was appointed manager of Middlesbrough, he was still refusing to talk to interviewers about the penalty which, sadly, is still regarded by many as the defining moment of his career.

The winner against Blackburn proved to be his only goal of what, not altogether surprisingly, proved to be a fairly low-key

1996-97 campaign for Gareth. Although Villa finished fifth, an ankle injury sustained against Wimbledon at Selhurst Park meant he was sidelined for seven games up to New Year and a further injury resulted in him missing a total of 11 games. He did, however, captain the team for the first time when Andy Townsend was ruled out of the 1-0 home defeat by Sheffield Wednesday at the end of January.

If that wasn't the best of starts as Villa skipper, there was a much happier tale when he took over on a more permanent basis in August. Little's men had just endured the worst start in their history – four straight defeats – and when Townsend was surprisingly sold to Middlesbrough on the day before Leeds United headed to Villa Park looking to make it five, Southgate was handed the captaincy.

It was an inspired choice. Villa stopped the rot thanks to a single Dwight Yorke goal and started to turn their season around with three straight league wins and progress against Girondins de Bordeaux in the UEFA Cup.

Although he missed a few games through injury around the turn of the year, Southgate, now an England regular, continued to lead by example on the pitch as well as displaying increasing maturity in dealing with off-the-field matters. Always a fair-minded individual, he had no hesitation in ticking off a team-mate who made a sexist remark to a female receptionist who had recently joined the staff at Bodymoor Heath.

Having taken over the captaincy just after Villa's worst-ever start, he was proud to lead the side to a record-breaking 12 league matches without defeat as they launched the 1998-99 campaign in stunning fashion and headed the Premiership table from mid-September until Boxing Day. It was almost illogical that the team should fare so well after the events of the previous summer, when Villa were beset by one problem after another, but it was certainly a time to savour.

"Our start that season was remarkable," says Southgate. "We

lost Dwight Yorke, who had been such a big player for us over the previous two seasons and no-one could have foreseen that we would go on such a good run. But we only conceded three goals in the first 10 matches and that was the basis of our success. And even though Dwight had gone, we bought Paul Merson and Dion Dublin, so it was an exciting squad again. In hindsight, we probably didn't have enough strength in depth to go on and become champions, but there was a great atmosphere around the place. Even so, I don't think we should have had a team picture taken on the pitch at Southampton after we had broken the record. I remember thinking at the time that it was the wrong thing to do. In my view, the club hadn't properly recognised Villa's European Cup triumph, although thankfully that's started to happen now, so to me it didn't mean a thing that we had merely made a good start. We were doing well but we had won nothing."

As if to mirror the captain's thoughts, Villa began to falter. For the first time since he had been at the club, Southgate felt the team had been let down by the defence as they conceded four goals at home to Liverpool in their first league defeat and then trailed 2-0 at Nottingham Forest before hitting back for a point.

However, even if the cracks were starting to show, Villa remained at the helm until early in the New Year, when striker Stan Collymore's depression and Ugo Ehiogu's serious eye injury contributed significantly to a lean spell which eventually saw them fall away to sixth. Maybe Collymore's extended absence was no great loss, because he had failed to live up to his club record £7m fee almost from the time he had arrived from Liverpool 18 months earlier.

But after Ehiogu damaged his eye socket at Newcastle at the end of January, Southgate was left with two inexperienced youngsters, Gareth Barry and Riccardo Scimeca, alongside him at the back. The strain began to show. Southgate scored the first own goal of his career in a 3-1 home defeat by Blackburn

as Villa went 10 matches without a win.

There was another own goal in the opening weeks of the following season, this time in a 3-1 defeat by Leicester City in a game which Gareth might just consider the most forgettable of his career. The obvious candidate might appear to be that Euro '96 semi-final against the Germans, but that hinged on a powder-puff penalty at the end of 120 minutes in which he had done precious little wrong. At Filbert Street on Saturday 25th September 1999, he did precious little right.

Once again, Villa had made a bright start and if it wasn't quite in the same league as 12 months earlier, they lay third in the table as they headed across to the East Midlands in optimistic mood. By the end of 90 nightmare minutes they were deflated and demoralised – and no-one more so than the skipper.

It was bad enough that he put the ball past Peter Enckelman for the Foxes' second goal; worse still that he was sent off for the first time in his career after being booked twice for fouls on Emile Heskey, a player whose awkward, unorthodox style was totally alien to a stylist like himself. Boss John Gregory argued later that the dismissal had been unfair, claiming Heskey had conned referee Jeff Winter into both cautions. Southgate, meanwhile, was so incensed that he uncharacteristically made a comment to the Cleveland official which later cost him a £5,000 fine.

"We had a really poor record against Leicester and I felt they were a team we should be beating," he says. "At half-time we were a goal down and I tried to get everybody going and asking more from them. Yet within three minutes of the re-start I had stuck the ball in my own net! It was a rousing speech, followed by a complete cock-up – and within 20 minutes I was sent off.

"Jeff Winter is a Middlesbrough fan and I see quite a lot of him. He's told me he thinks he got it wrong because both fouls were 50-50 and he booked me for both. But that doesn't excuse what I said to him when he sent me off. The embarrassment of having done what I did at half-time and then having to go off really got to me and I reacted in the wrong way. The FA were quite right to fine me. I learned a lesson that day which has stuck with me."

The defeat by Martin O'Neill's team was a setback which had far-reaching consequences as Villa embarked on a dismal run of nine league matches without a win, and speculation mounted over Gregory's job. By early December the team had plunged to 15th in the table, and it was unquestionably the nadir for both manager and captain when they were beaten on penalties in a League Cup quarter-final at West Ham.

Three-and-a-half years after his fateful miss against Germany at Wembley, Southgate contrived to fail again from 12 yards in another corner of London. This time it was Shaka Hislop who saved the crucial penalty as Villa's season plunged from one crisis to another.

A gutted Gareth and his dejected team-mates must have been convinced the whole world was against them that Wednesday night as they headed back up the M1. Little could they have known that within 48 hours, their rapidly-sinking season would be thrown a lifeline – without a football in sight.

When I made a routine call to secretary Steve Stride on the Friday afternoon, I hardly expected the piece of information he gave me. The club were demanding re-entry into the League Cup because West Ham had fielded an ineligible player at Upton Park. Emmanuel Omoyinmi, who had gone on as substitute for the final six minutes of extra time, had already appeared in the competition while on loan at Gillingham and was therefore cup-tied.

Villa's appeal was upheld, with the Football League ordering that the tie should be re-staged in January. No-one was more relieved than Gareth Southgate that his latest penalty howler would, along with the rest of the match, be declared void and expunged from the record books. And he recalls vividly how he heard the news.

"John (Gregory) came to my house to tell me we were back in, which was an incredible story," he says. "But when he turned up, I thought he had come to tell me he had got the sack! He was under the cosh at the time because results were nowhere near as good as we had hoped. As captain, I felt a big responsibility for that. My penalty miss had cost us the match at West Ham and I already felt as low as I possibly could.

"Fortunately, it was good news that John gave me that day, and Doug Ellis and the board were rewarded for remaining patient with him. We reached the semi-finals of the League Cup when the match at Upton Park was re-staged and later got to the FA Cup final."

Villa's season, in fact, was back on course just three days after the match that never was. Despite the dreadful news that Dion Dublin had broken his neck, a 2-1 home win over Sheffield Wednesday provided the springboard for a 12-match unbeaten Premiership run which carried Villa to sixth, the position in which they would eventually finish.

It was heady stuff, particularly as they also reached the FA Cup final for the first time since 1957. As captain, Southgate had the honour of leading Villa up the tunnel and out on to the Wembley turf for the last final to be played beneath the twin towers and it is a moment which will remain with him forever, despite defeat by Chelsea in one of the most boring matches to be staged at the famous old stadium.

"It was a really poor game and we didn't go into it with enough belief," he says. "But there were things going on behind the scenes. Merse was unsettled and Benito Carbone, who was with us on a short-term contract, learned that he wasn't going to be kept on after the final. Those things certainly didn't help our preparation, although Chelsea also had much more experience of big games. It was a fair result but if you ask any of the players in the Villa team, they will tell you what a big regret it is that we didn't perform on the day."

While cup finals invariably stick in the mind, his more enduring memories of the Millennium must surely be of the first few days of 2000. In four-and-a-half seasons until then, he had contributed a grand total of four goals to the Villa cause. In the space of six days, totally without warning, he added three more. I make no excuse for reproducing the opening paragraphs of my *Birmingham Post* match report from Villa's New Year Bank Holiday victory away to Leeds United:

'Anyone who predicted Gareth Southgate would score Aston Villa's first goal of the new century would have been accused of having a drop too much over the festive season. The suggestion that the England defender might grab two in one match might have been regarded as near-impossible. And the notion that a Southgate brace would help Villa to launch the year 2000 with an away victory over Premiership leaders Leeds United would have been dismissed as sheer fantasy. Yet all those things came to pass on an incredible afternoon at Elland Road.'

His manager, for one, was completely taken aback by the fact that Southgate should score twice in one match, making the point that his dependable centre-back was known as "the ornament" because of his penchant for going forward at every corner but never actually making contact with the ball!

Well, this time he did, even if neither contact was exactly convincing. The first, a scuffed shot after he had initially headed down a Paul Merson corner, barely managed to cross the line. The second, a stooping header from a Merson free-kick, slipped just beyond goalkeeper Nigel Martyn's reach and crept inside the far post.

Afterwards, Gareth couldn't help recalling that the only previous time he had scored twice in one game had been against Villa. He admitted, too, that his brace at Leeds were "two of the worst goals you could wish to see."

Five days later he was at it again, nodding in from point-blank range to secure a fourth round FA Cup passage at the expense of Southampton after Ian Taylor had headed on a Paul Merson free-kick. Ironically, the combined distance for Villa's first three goals of the year was roughly 12 yards – the distance which had been such a psychological barrier at Wembley and West Ham.

Such was his buoyant mood after the match, that he said he would be willing to offer his services from the penalty spot, if required, for the re-staged League Cup clash at Upton Park three days later. The raised eyebrows of reporters who were interviewing him said it all – hold on a minute Gareth, let's not get carried away! In the event, he was able to concentrate on defensive duties as the Hammers were beaten 3-1 after extra time, although his trio of goals against Leeds and Southampton almost certainly played a part in him being named January's Premiership Player of the Month.

It was an eventful season, culminating in the FA Cup final, but it also took its toll on Southgate, both physically and mentally. A virtual ever-present since his arrival from Palace, he had been denied a holiday for the previous four summers and with the European Championship finals looming, this year was going to be no different. There was clearly a danger of burn-out, which was why Gregory rested him for consecutive games against Tottenham and Leicester City in April. The manager even went as far as banning his captain from the training ground for 10 days, insisting: "There's only so much the body can take and Gareth badly needs a breather. He can stay at home or go on holiday but I don't want to see him."

That enforced break helped to ensure Southgate was fit and well to report for Kevin Keegan's Euro 2000 squad. It also gave him time to contemplate his future, and the fax he sent Villa just before heading off to Holland and Belgium with England was the last thing the club wanted. He was asking for a transfer.

'It has not been an easy decision but my mind is made up,' he wrote. 'This is something I have been thinking about for the last few months. I have given everything to Villa over the last five years, but if I am to achieve what I want to achieve in my career, it's time for a move.'

Typically, there was nothing underhand about the manner in which Gareth Southgate made his request to leave, just an honest statement about how he felt, which makes it all the more mystifying that he has subsequently been subjected to such vitriol from some supporters on his returns to Villa Park. Not that all Villa fans hold a grudge against him. "I can't fathom why a long-serving captain gets the bird whenever he returns," says Ian Bourne of Lichfield. "All he said was what a lot of fans had been saying all along – and he served us with honour for six years." And Richard Whitehead asks: "What exactly did he do wrong? Our very own Captain Sensible was a leading member of Villa's best Premiership team and he never, ever let anyone down. It was a measure of the man that his best season in claret and blue was his final one."

That perfectly sums up Southgate. There were strong rumours that his mind was set on a move to Chelsea and the Londoners, did, indeed, make three bids for him during the course of the summer. When Villa rejected all of them Southgate didn't sulk, like many players might have done. He simply buckled down to what must be one of the longest goodbyes in football history.

It was more than a year before he finally left – to Teesside, rather than Thames-side – and during that time he was as professional as ever against a backdrop of claim and counter claim about whether or not he still wanted to get away. Only the man himself knew the answer to that, but barely a month passed without one of his team-mates either pleading with him to stay or urging the club to find a way of getting him to stick around.

George Boateng, who also eventually moved to Middlesbrough, was among those who lobbied for Villa to avoid the departure of their classy centre-back. In an article in the *Sunday Mercury*, the Dutch midfielder left no-one in any doubt about his feelings. 'Gareth is without question one of the best defenders in the Premiership,' he said. 'Keeping him is vital if we are serious about heading to the top. Gareth is a huge player for this club. You just have to look at our record when he is out of the team to see what a massive impact he has. If we are serious about building towards a Champions League place over the next three years, he has to be at the heart of the team.'

Southgate's resolve to leave, unfortunately, was as strong as ever, although he never allowed it to interfere with his form. Once again, his performances were as consistent as ever and it was significant that when he missed seven matches after falling awkwardly in an FA Cup replay against Newcastle United, the defence did not look as assured. Villa recorded only a single victory during that period; they were unbeaten in six following his return to the line-up.

He chipped in with a couple more goals, too, opening the scoring in the home match against Bradford City in September and heading home from close range in a 2-1 win at Leeds just before Christmas. Considering his goal tally for the club amounted to a fairly modest nine, Leeds must have felt victimised to think he reserved a third of his total for them!

Once again, though, he derived his greatest satisfaction from being part of a defence which provided Villa with a solid base as they finished a respectable eighth. But a parting of the ways was becoming increasingly inevitable, particularly after he asked to be relieved of the captaincy for the final match of the season at St. James's Park. It certainly wasn't a farewell to cherish, Villa crashing 3-0 to Newcastle and Southgate picking up a booking. What an inappropriately sad end to a distinguished career in claret and blue for the man who was a template for the term "model pro."

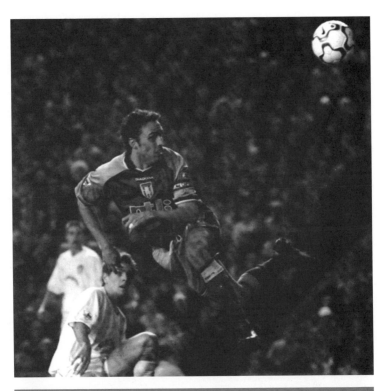

GARETH SOUTHGATE - CAREER STATS

BORN:	Watford
DATE OF BIRTH:	September 3 1970
JOINED VILLA:	July 1995
VILLA LEAGUE APPS:	191
GOALS:	7
VILLA CUP APPS:	51
GOALS	2
INT. CAPS (England):	57
GOALS:	2

Paul
Merson

'Let's get this straight, Merse. You're happy to talk about drink, drugs and gambling, but not about food?'

This was the question I formed in my mind, although it never passed my lips. The actual words which came out were rather less confrontational. "Right, Paul," I said. "Let's move on to the next one."

Paul Merson, self-confessed alcoholic, drug-addict and gambler, had been talking openly about his former habits as we conducted a question-and-answer session for the *Villa News & Record*. Yet when I raised the subject of dining out, he suddenly clammed up. It was, indeed, a bizarre interview, one which remains as vivid in my memory as any of the brilliant performances he served up during almost four years as a Villa player. It went like this:

Is there anything you couldn't live without?
Sanity. After all the problems I've had over the years, I've come to realise just how important that is.
What's the bravest thing you've ever done?
Gone into treatment for alcoholism.
What is the best book you've ever read?
A big blue book called *Alcoholics Anonymous*. It saved my life.

Merse even joked, when asked if he was influenced by

television advertising: "They don't advertise cocaine on television, do they?" That flippant response, needless to say, didn't make it into the Villa programme. Yet while he was happy to talk about such serious issues and had previously been candid about his divorce and contemplating suicide in interviews I'd conducted for the *Birmingham Post*, he suddenly had a problem when I asked what seemed to be a perfectly harmless question:

What's the most expensive meal you've ever had?

"I don't think I should answer that" was his curt reply, which is why we moved quickly on. Just why he was unwilling to talk about going out for a meal, and how much it cost, was mystifying in the extreme. But I wasn't complaining. During his time at Villa Park, Merse gave tremendous value to any reporter who cared to sit down and talk to him – and even better value to those who paid to watch him play football. Villa fans took him to their hearts like few other Holte End heroes, and retained their affection for him after he left. That much was evident when he scored against Villa, just before the start of the 2003-04 campaign.

Ask any footballer to nominate his "dream goal" and you're likely to get a description of a stunning 30-yard volley, a diving header, a sublime lob, an overhead kick or a breathtaking solo run. Alternatively, some players might bring to mind a more simple effort which proved to be a Cup final winner. Peter Withe, for instance, never scored a more memorable goal than his miscued shot which made Villa champions of Europe in 1982. Yet when Merson scored his dream goal 21 years later, it was in a friendly rather than a final, and it was as ordinary a goal as you will ever see.

If the game was of no consequence, though, and the goal an untidy stab from no more than eight yards, Merse must have thought he was dreaming as 3,000 opposition supporters leapt from their seats and gave him a standing ovation. And just in case he felt like pinching himself at such a rapturous reception, the visiting contingent repeated the accolade when his name was announced over the PA system.

The surreal situation unfolded at Bescot Stadium when he scored for Walsall against the club who had released him 12 months earlier. In the interim period, Merse had helped Portsmouth to reach the Premiership for the first time, and maybe if he'd stayed at Fratton Park and scored against Villa on the opening day of the Premiership season, the reception from travelling fans would have been more muted.

With no real harm done by his goal for the Saddlers, though, the Villa faithful were only too happy to acclaim a player they had idolised for the best part of four seasons.

Indeed, supporters had been deeply unhappy over manager Graham Taylor's decision to let Merson leave, but if that transfer was down to the manager, it had been a rather different scenario when Merse arrived at Villa Park from Middlesbrough in September 1998.

There can be any number of reasons why a player moves from one club to another, the most common being that he has simply been made a better offer. But that certainly wasn't the case when Merse switched from Teesside to the Midlands. He claimed a 'drinking culture' had evolved at The Riverside and as a recovering alcoholic, he argued, he simply couldn't risk the temptation of being dragged into it. He was no stranger to the demon drink, nor was it his only vice, having also been addicted to gambling and cocaine during a few hazy years at Arsenal before seeking help to clean up his act.

If his personal life was frequently in turmoil, though, he was a class act as a footballer. He was 30 by the time he arrived at Villa Park so his £6.75m transfer fee wasn't exactly cheap, but the club undeniably got a good return on their investment as he exhibited his visionary midfield skills in claret and blue before taking the road to Walsall via the south coast.

But we're racing ahead of ourselves here, just as Paul Merson often seemed to do. Born in Northolt, Middlesex in 1968, he joined Arsenal as a trainee in 1984 and made his first-team debut two years later. By 1989, he experienced the dizzy heights of a Championship campaign, helping the Gunners to a dramatic title triumph with 10 goals in 37 league appearances. It was a classic case of too much, too soon. By the following year his off-the-field problems had begun to surface and at one stage he was banned from Highbury amid reports of drinking and gambling debts.

The 1990-91 campaign saw an upturn in his fortunes as he scored 16 goals and collected another championship medal, and a year later he made his full England debut under Graham Taylor, who included him in the 1992 European Championship squad.

The honours continued to roll in. In 1993, the Gunners enjoyed an FA Cup and League Cup double, the following year there was European Cup Winners' Cup glory. But all the time his darker side was lurking and in November 1994 he confessed to his cocaine habit and was admitted to an addiction unit.

In 1997, having been at Arsenal for 13 years, he joined Middlesbrough and helped them to promotion. He could hardly have imagined that 12 months later he would be on the move once again.

He was actually in action at Villa Park two-and-a-half weeks before John Gregory secured his signature, playing for Middlesbrough in Villa's first match AD – After Dwight.

Yorke had been sold to Manchester United a few days earlier and Villa were in turmoil. Chairman Doug Ellis had been subjected to constant vitriol at the club's annual meeting, the timing of which could not have been worse. It was on a Thursday evening just hours after Yorke had been unveiled at Old Trafford, and shareholders queued in the aisles to let Ellis know exactly what they thought about him selling the team's most valuable and best-loved player.

Little could they have known the signing of a new hero was only a couple of weeks away. If things were far from happy in Villa's world right then, Merson wasn't jumping for joy either. Despite Boro's elevation to the top flight, he had become unsettled on Teesside and he posed no threat whatsoever as Villa won 3-1 to register their 100th Premiership victory.

No-one presumed anything on the strength of one result, but the good times were about to roll again for Villa. They had just embarked on what was to be the club's best-ever start to a league season, and one of the game's most creative exponents was about to join them.

In fitting with such big signing – second only to the £7m Villa had paid Liverpool for Stan Collymore the previous year – there was a sense of pure theatre about the press conference which was staged to herald Merson's arrival.

These events are invariably late starting but on this occasion the assembled media had to wait for the duration of a football match before the new signing emerged, flanked by chairman Doug Ellis and manager John Gregory. Around 60 fans who had waited outside for a glimpse of Merse were then invited inside to swell the massed ranks of reporters, photographers and cameramen. And just as the proceedings were getting under way, we were interrupted by loud music which blasted across the stadium as tests were carried out on the Public Address system. There was, for sure, a circus atmosphere to the grand event, the like of which had never previously been witnessed at a Villa press conference.

Merson had signed too late to play in the 1-0 home victory over Newcastle United 24 hours later so it was the following Saturday, against Wimbledon, that he pulled on the No 10 claret and blue shirt for the first time. It was love at first sight as far as Villa supporters were concerned. They desperately craved a new idol to replace the departed Yorke and were convinced from Merson's first touch – a superb pass on the turn – that they had found just the man.

He marked his debut with a goal in a 2-0 win, too, although it was hardly one to savour. The sequence of events which led up to it, in fact, was extremely confusing. Lee Hendrie had scored the only goal against Newcastle from the spot three days earlier but when Villa were awarded a penalty in the 33rd minute against the Dons, Gregory indicated that Alan Thompson, the club's £4.5m signing from Bolton Wanderers, should take the kick. It wasn't a wise decision, the Geordie midfielder sending his shot wide of the left-hand post. So when Villa were awarded another penalty on the stroke of half-time, Merson took it upon himself to assume the responsibility. He, too, nearly made a mess of it, goalkeeper Neil Sullivan saving as he dived to his left, but Merse got lucky, nudging home the rebound before he was engulfed by jubilant team-mates. Ian Taylor scored the second goal 12 minutes into the second half, and the new boy was off to a winning start.

Things could hardly have gone any better during the next few weeks. Although Merson was ineligible for the club's UEFA Cup ties, he continued to have a major influence on the domestic front. He netted the only goal against Derby and even though he missed a sitter in a goalless draw at West Ham, the fans were more than happy to excuse him as Villa maintained their unbeaten league run. The sequence was extended to 11 when Dion Dublin, newly-recruited from Coventry City for £5.75m, marked his debut with two goals in a 3-2 home win over Tottenham.

That result equalled the club's best start to a league campaign since 1932 and the following week they created a piece of club history by taking it to 12 with an emphatic 4-1 success at Southampton. Dublin netted a hat-trick at The Dell but Merson also made an important contribution with a sublime

77th-minute goal, sweeping the ball home on the run to round off an incisive end-to-end move which was instigated by Gareth Barry's long diagonal pass and continued by Collymore's low centre.

Those were heady days indeed, for Villa in general and Merson in particular. At Wembley the following Wednesday, the club's feel-good factor was transferred to the international stage as Dublin set up Merson for a goal in England's 2-0 win over the Czech Republic, and Hendrie also went close to scoring after going on as a late substitute. It was the first time for 67 years that three Villa players had been involved in the same England match. For Eric Houghton, Joe Tate and Pongo Waring against Belgium in 1931 read Merson, Dublin and Hendrie against the Czechs in 1998.

If Merse felt at that juncture that life couldn't get any better, he was absolutely right. Liverpool inflicted Villa's first league defeat of the season with a 4-2 verdict at Villa Park three days later and the following week's 2-2 draw at Nottingham Forest proved to be his last for nearly two months. He had been nursing a back problem for some time and the game at the City Ground was one too many. He openly admitted at half-time that he was unable to play on, and has since described his first-half performance, as Villa went two-down, as "pathetic and embarrassing."

He might also have used the same words for the events of the next eight weeks. During his lengthy lay-off, without the focus of match day, he became disillusioned and even considered retirement. Worse still, he slipped back into his gambling habits and incurred the wrath of manager Gregory by jetting off to New York for a weekend to watch an ice hockey match and an American football game. As Gregory told him later, it wasn't flying to the States that was the issue, but the fact that he hadn't informed anyone at the club.

There were plenty of things Paul Merson didn't tell the club about over the next few months. Although he regained fitness and returned to the Villa line-up, his private life was in utter turmoil. He gambled even more heavily, started drinking again and rowed constantly with his wife Lorraine, from whom he was later divorced. Such was his mental state that he even cried in front of Gregory on one occasion and later broke down when he was convinced the rest of the team had turned against him. There were times, even, when he was suicidal. He admitted as much the following April, when he publicly bared his soul as Villa prepared for their FA Cup semi-final against Bolton Wanderers at Wembley.

"The semi-final will be a year since I took my last drink and wanted to kill myself," he told a group of reporters as we chatted outside the old Trinity Road stand after a 2-0 home victory over Derby County. "I didn't think I had another recovery in me. But I didn't stop drinking, taking drugs and gambling to play football. That wasn't the deal. I did it to spend quality time with my kids. They can be proud of their dad today."

Indeed they could. The fact that Villa had reached the semi-finals of the Cup was a fair indication of just how much the team's – and Merson's – fortunes had been revived since the slump at the end of the previous season, although it wasn't a straightforward turnaround. Merse didn't make the starting line-up for the first four matches and it wasn't until the home match against Sheffield Wednesday a week before Christmas that his season really took off. Even then, he contrived to miss a penalty as Pavel Srnicek saved his spot-kick, but his goal in a 2-1 victory was one for the connoisseur, a curling shot from the edge of the penalty area which left the goalkeeper helpless. The 68th-minute effort was scored with the aplomb of a player whose team were several goals ahead, rather than desperately seeking an equaliser, and from that juncture, Merse was a revelation. The victory, sadly, was overshadowed by a collision which resulted in Dion Dublin needing surgery on a broken neck, but it was undoubtedly the turning point of Merson's campaign.

Earlier in the season, he had revealed a desire to move into management – something he claims he would have done there and then had the opportunity presented itself – but suddenly his mind was focused purely on extending a brilliant career. Between the victory over Wednesday in December and the FA Cup final the following May, he missed just one game, the return match against the Owls at Hillsborough. And while he was frequently withdrawn from games during the initial stages of that impressive run, he was clearly getting stronger and more influential all the time.

Maybe there had been times when Gregory questioned his own judgment in persuading Villa to outlay so much money on a player battling against so many private demons, but as time progressed the manager had every reason to feel satisfied with the business he had conducted on the club's behalf.

Merson produced some of the finest football of his career during those few months as Villa climbed to sixth in the table, reached the League Cup semi-finals and made their first appearance in the FA Cup final since winning the trophy in 1957. The big occasion, sadly, was one to forget as Gregory's boys simply never got going and slipped to a 1-0 defeat to Chelsea in the last final to be played at the old Wembley Stadium. Merse was no better and no worse than any of his team-mates on that bitterly disappointing afternoon, but his Wembley woe should not detract from his wonderful displays throughout the second half of the season.

He was invariably Villa's star performer, and while several of his colleagues were also impressive in that five-month period, it was no great surprise to anyone when he won both the supporters' and players' Player of the Year titles. It got to the stage, in fact, where his role as the pivotal figure in a hugely successful run was almost taken for granted, very much like

Paul McGrath's defensive dependability had been a few years earlier.

But even in the midst of near perfection, there were times when his game was somehow elevated to an ever higher level, none more so than the fifth round Cup tie against Leeds United at the end of January. In many ways, you could draw a parallel with a famous game at Wembley in 1953, a game which has become etched in football folklore as the 'Matthews' Final', even though it was Stan Mortensen who scored the hat-trick which gave Blackpool a 4-3 triumph over Bolton Wanderers. At Villa Park on 30th January, 2000, Benito Carbone was given an idea of how Mortensen must have felt all those years before. The Italian striker also netted a hat-trick as Villa, twice behind, hit back to win 3-2, but it was very much 'Merson's Match'.

Almost half a century after Stanley Matthews' wing wizardry had bemused Bolton, Merse's magic left Leeds in a right old spin. Having relentlessly teased and tormented the then Premiership title contenders, he wasn't even on the pitch for the final 20 minutes of a pulsating tie, but by then he had done enough to see Villa through to the quarter-finals. Not that he was aware of the fact.

His most vital contribution was a deft flick forwards from the edge of the penalty area, followed by a second touch across goal for Carbone to head what proved to be the winning goal. As the Italian milked the rapturous applause from ecstatic Holte Enders, Merson was oblivious to the celebrations, having been knocked out by a clash of heads with Leeds defender Michael Duberry as he made the crucial second contact.

After four minutes of treatment to a blood-gushing head wound, it became apparent that there was no way he – or Duberry – could continue. As the final stages of a dramatic contest unfolded, the duo were being patched up in the medical room, neither of them realising the significance of the head-to-head encounter which had left them concussed.

Leaning across to enquire about Merson's welfare, Duberry joked: "At least I stopped you scoring!" It was only when Villa's medical officer Barrie Smith joined in the conversation that the bruised and battered rivals became aware of what had transpired.

That combination of brilliance and bravery took Merson's stock to new heights and it continued to climb as he followed up by being voted the Premiership Player of the Month for February. Despite everything he had achieved at Highbury, the first half of 2000 was arguably the peak of his career. His team-mates frequently commented that he was playing better than ever, and while the Leeds match was undoubtedly the most memorable of Villa's season, it was by no means the only occasion when he had supporters drooling over his poise and panache.

He had missed the previous season's trip to Middlesbrough, but made a triumphant return to The Riverside on Valentine's Day as Villa thrashed his former club 4-0. He made way for Lee Hendrie just past the hour mark that night, but not before totally outshining Boro's Paul Gascoigne, Paul Ince and Juninho in the battle for midfield supremacy.

Then there was a 4-2 win over Tottenham at White Hart Lane, made all the sweeter by the fact that he was captain in the absence of the injured Gareth Southgate. Not surprisingly, he was given a hostile reception because of his association with Spurs' north London rivals Arsenal, but took great satisfaction in helping Villa to victory after they had gone two-down just after half-time.

That wasn't the first time he had been made skipper. He had also been handed the armband for the home match against Watford in early February, responding to the extra responsibility with a quality display and two outstanding goals in a 4-0 win. Gregory recognised that his midfield maestro was not only playing some of the best football of his life, he also commanded respect from the rest of the players.

As I observed in the *Birmingham Post* around that time: "If there is one certainty for Aston Villa these days, it is a guaranteed performance from Paul Merson. At 31, fatigue is always likely to take its toll at any stage from half-time onwards. While he is on the pitch, though, he simply oozes quality and, more important, his indisputable craft is now allied to non-stop graft. Merson's name is first on the team sheet for most matches." Apart from producing the brush strokes of an artist, he was also working tirelessly as a painter and decorator.

Even on the occasional off day, he still managed to make an impact. If the fifth-round tie against Leeds had been a personal triumph, the sixth-round visit to Everton was largely one to forget for Merse. He was anonymous for most of the first half and was replaced by Ian Taylor for the second – but not before he had been instrumental in both goals in a 2-1 victory!

"I wasn't angry at being brought off," he said later. "The boss said he was going to make a change and I was okay with that. I helped create the goals and he said to me: 'You have won us the game.' I totally understand the reasons for being brought off."

Things weren't always quite that smooth, of course. The relationship between manager and player was very much one of the love-hate variety. Sometimes everything was sweetness and light, on other occasions they were at each other's throats. Merse, for instance, was an unlikely ally for his boss when the manager's job was under threat following a return of just two points from a possible 18 towards the end of 1999. At the time, the midfielder was frustrated at not being able to command a regular place but he made it clear the blame lay with the players rather than the manager.

In total contrast, he blew his top after being replaced at half-time in a defeat at Southampton the following season, and was later overheard saying to a friend on his mobile phone:

"After the row we've had, I don't know if I will play for this club again."

But there was humour, too. After receiving treatment on the touchline in one match, Merson was about to return to the pitch when he took a phone call from Gregory, who was sitting in the directors' box, on the dug-out telephone. The likelihood is that the pair briefly discussed tactics but when Gregory was asked what the conversation had entailed, he replied: "Paul asked what had won the 3.30!"

If his relationship with the manager was sometimes uneasy, Merse equally had no qualms about speaking out against his playing colleagues. Having blamed them for the club's bleak midwinter, he clearly wasn't impressed to hear that Benito Carbone, who had signed from Sheffield Wednesday on a short-term contract in October, was demanding a weekly wage of £33,000 to extend his employment in claret and blue beyond the end of that season. The club's top earners, Merson included, were on around £20,000, and chairman Doug Ellis was reticent to upset them by giving Carbone nearly 60 per cent more.

"It's nothing to do with me," Merse insisted, but you just knew he was going to share his opinion with anyone who cared to listen. "Villa are surely not going to break their pay structure?" he added. "If it was someone like Dennis Bergkamp, maybe they would have to think about it, but I don't think you can break the structure to that extent. I can see the chairman's point of view 100 per cent. I like Beni. He's a very good player and you need top quality players if you are going to win things. But if it gets into the sort of scenario we are talking about, it gets ridiculous."

The Board clearly agreed. A goal at Wembley on Cup final day might have persuaded them otherwise, but three minutes after his countryman Roberto Di Matteo had scored for Chelsea, Carbone wasted a glorious chance to equalise, scuffing his shot embarrassingly wide from 12 yards when he was completely unmarked.

While Carbone headed off into the sunset, Merson confirmed that he was remaining a Villa player. Rumours had surfaced that he was unsettled and wanted to leave but when Villa were welcomed home on the day after their Cup final defeat, he earned the biggest cheer of the afternoon in Birmingham's Centenary Square when he announced his intention to stay. His popularity was perfectly understandable, too. Quite apart from the delightful manner in which he played football, he was equally charming whenever he came into contact with supporters, particularly the younger fans. As a kid, he had once been snubbed by one of his Chelsea idols after asking for an autograph. He had vowed never to treat his own admirers with such disdain. He was also determined to remain in peak condition. Spurred on by the arrival of Belgian striker Luc Nilis and flamboyant French winger David Ginola, he trained every day that summer.

For all that, he had to come to terms with the disappointment of being omitted from the England squad for the Euro 2000 finals – and was then thrust back into action for Villa in mid-July. The club's decision to compete in the Intertoto Cup meant they were down to competitive business five weeks before the Premiership season opened, and Merse must have wished he was on the beach.

After having an effort disallowed for handball in the first leg against Marila Pribram in the Czech Republic, he was sent off for two bookable offences in the return match, staged at The Hawthorns because of work on Villa Park's new Trinity Road stand. It was certainly an inauspicious start to the new campaign, but it was to get better. And while he never quite attained the heights of the previous season, he once again walked off with a Player of the Year double.

Such was his ability to turn a game that his manager went as far as claiming the rest of the side relied too heavily on him. After he had orchestrated a 2-1 home win over Charlton Athletic on a rain-sodden surface, Gregory complained: "They tend to look at him and say 'do something special, Merse.' They want him to score a goal from nothing but sometimes I think we put too much responsibility on his shoulders."

Merson not only scored the second goal that day, he also proved he was just as creative in monsoon conditions as on billiard table surfaces, prompting Graham Hill of the *Sunday Mercury* to suggest that "you might as well put Merson's name on the Man of the Match award before the game has even started."

The man himself wasn't inclined to disagree. "John Gregory says I'm playing better now than in my trophy-winning days with Arsenal," he said. "I think he's right. I'm 32 now but that's just a number. When I was 21, I couldn't get out of bed in the morning because I'd been drinking the night before."

He also reached an important milestone that season, netting the 100th league goal of his career in a 4-1 drubbing of Derby County, and by the end of October he had been handed a contract extension designed to keep him at Villa Park until the summer of 2003.

A couple of days later he produced his super show against Charlton and the following weekend he scored one of the most audacious goals you will ever witness. In between times, he had struck the bar from 30 yards in a 1-0 League Cup defeat at home to Manchester City but at soggy Goodison Park on Bonfire Night, he added a late touch of sparkle to a match which had previously been a damp squib. A dreadful contest had just entered its final minute and everyone was resigned to a goalless draw until Merson spotted Paul Gerrard off his line and sent a 35-yard lob over the goalkeeper's head and into the net.

It was one of half-a-dozen goals he scored that season, the last of them the winner against Midland neighbours Coventry

City in the final home match. Villa were two-down at the interval to a brace from Moroccan Moustapha Hadji, who would join them by the start of the following season. But Darius Vassell reduced the deficit, Juan Pablo Angel equalised with his first goal for the club and with six minutes remaining, Merson curled home a 25-yarder which secured a dramatic 3-2 win and condemned Coventry to relegation.

Along with Villa 'keeper David James, Merse also finished 2000-01 with the rare distinction of being a Premiership ever-present, although, typically, he derived no great sense of pride from the achievement. Instead, after the shambles of a 3-0 defeat at Newcastle in the final game, he used the statistic to underline, in his usual outspoken fashion, why he felt Villa were not about to challenge the Premier League's elite.

"The fact that I've played in every game says it all," he said. "It wouldn't happen at clubs like Manchester United, Arsenal or Liverpool, where the squad rotation system means they can juggle with 20 players every week. If you have the same team, you are going to get the same position – eighth or ninth. This is a nice club, I'm afraid. The players are a lovely bunch of lads, but great lads are not going to put any trophies in the cabinet."

As it happened, just three months later Villa's lovely bunch of lads did put a trophy in the cabinet - with Merson at the helm. In the wake of Gareth Southgate's departure to Middlesbrough, he was appointed captain as Villa made another early start in the Intertoto Cup. And after overcoming Croatians Slaven Belupo and French club Stade Rennais, Villa lifted the trophy with a 5-2 aggregate victory over Basel in the final. The new skipper scored in the 1-1 first-leg draw in Switzerland, too, and although he watched the return match from the substitutes' bench, he was later pictured at the front of a jubilant team group, wearing a tracksuit and a huge grin and clutching the tiny cup in his left hand.

His captaincy also coincided with an encouraging start to the league campaign, featuring draws against Tottenham and Manchester United and a 3-1 success at Liverpool, where Villa had previously won only twice in 22 visits. It was late October, in fact, before Gregory's men suffered their first league setback, a 3-2 defeat at Everton – and seven days later they sat proudly at the top of the table after consecutive home wins over Charlton and Bolton.

But Merson's forecast that Villa would be unable to sustain a challenge to the big boys ultimately came to pass. The club parted company with Gregory in January and Villa finished eighth for the second year running. It was a low-key season for Merson, too, injuries restricting him to just 18 league starts and three substitute appearances. In the midst of a generally disappointing season, though, he at least had the satisfaction of scoring against Arsenal at Highbury and was also on target in the 1-1 home draw against his boyhood favourites Chelsea in the game which launched Graham Taylor's second spell as manager. He was hardly involved, however, as the season petered out to a tame conclusion and it was no great surprise when he was released on a free transfer at the start of the following season, making his only Villa appearance as a substitute in the second leg of an Intertoto tie against Zurich.

We will never know how things might have turned out if he had stayed, but he certainly enjoyed a happier 2002-03 season than the team-mates he left behind, using all his guile, vision and experience to steer Portsmouth to promotion while Taylor's side spluttered to a finishing position of 16th. But at least the claret and blue army had one last chance to salute him when he headed back to the Midlands and scored for Walsall against Villa in that pre-season friendly at the Bescot.

He would have relished the moment, too. Despite all his off-the-field problems, he was essentially a guy whose greatest desire was to play football, regardless of the surroundings. A few weeks after playing for Villa in the 2000 FA Cup final at Wembley, for instance, he was driving home one afternoon when he spotted a group of youngsters kicking a ball around on a grassed area in the Kingstanding area of Birmingham. Jumpers had been thrown down to act as goalposts and it was a far cry from Wembley, but he simply couldn't resist the lure of the game. He stopped the car, jumped out and asked if he could join in. For the rest of their lives, those kids will be able to talk about the day Paul Merson asked them for a game.

PAUL MERSON - CAREER STATS	
BORN:	Harlesden
DATE OF BIRTH:	March 20 1968
JOINED VILLA:	September 1998
VILLA LEAGUE APPS:	117
GOALS:	18
VILLA CUP APPS:	27
GOALS	1
INT. CAPS (England):	21
GOALS:	3

1998-2004

Dion
Dublin

The rest of the pitch was deserted as Dion Dublin stood in the centre-circle, his arms raised in acknowledgement of rapturous applause from every corner of Villa Park. He had hardly kicked a ball in anger for three months and soon he would be on his way to fresh pastures after being released by manager David O'Leary. But there was no way he was going to leave without a proper send-off. Ian Taylor, another of Villa's favourite sons, had been allowed to slip away almost unnoticed 12 months earlier. The club weren't about to make the same mistake again.

Dublin hadn't started a match since early February so it was no great surprise that he was only on the substitutes' bench for the final game of the season against Manchester United. But after replacing Gareth Barry eight minutes from time, he joined the rest of the team on a traditional lap of honour in front of the capacity crowd. Then, while the rest of the players retreated to the dressing room, Dublin returned to the middle of the pitch to answer the call for an encore from more than 15,000 fans who had remained in the ground to show their appreciation one last time.

At that moment, he was a man alone but also a man with thousands of friends. If he'd had his saxophone with him, the accomplished musician would most likely have given them a tune. For nearly six years, he had done everything but.

Dion Dublin would never claim to be Villa's greatest striker but his contribution to the cause over five-and-a-half years was immense. Here was a man who broke his neck for the claret and blue cause, a man whose ebullient personality lit up the Villa dressing room as well as the terraces, a man with great leadership qualities. More than anyone else, he was an inspiration to the club's younger players, who frequently sought his advice and guidance.

And if he wasn't the most prolific scorer to pull on a Villa shirt, he was unquestionably the most explosive. It didn't quite register with most of us at the time, but there had never been a start to a Villa career quite like the one Dublin made in November 1998.

Two goals at home to Tottenham on his debut were followed by a hat-trick at Southampton, then two more against Liverpool. Never in the history of Aston Villa had any player scored seven goals in his first three league games, not even Jasper McLukie, who netted seven in four way back in 1901.

That was 87 years before Dion Dublin began his professional career with Norwich City. Although his first spell at Carrow Road lasted barely five months, he made his name with the goals which steered Cambridge United to the FA Cup quarter-finals in 1990 and earned him a £1m move to Manchester United two years later. Sadly, a broken leg restricted him to just 17 games in two years at Old Trafford but he followed that with 169 appearances and 72 goals for Coventry City before his £5.75m transfer to Villa.

More than a few eyebrows were raised when he moved across the Midlands, not so much because of the size of the fee but because of the length of his contract. Villa did, indeed, appear to be taking something of a gamble by offering a five-year deal to a 29-year-old so it was no great surprise when the issue was brought up at the press conference to announce his arrival. But manager John Gregory, who was rarely lost for words, had the perfect answer. "When Dion gets fed up playing centre-forward", said the manager, "he can go and play centre-half."

Dublin had already displayed an aptitude for the defensive side of the game during his time with the Sky Blues and, as Gregory predicted, he would do so for his new club a little further down the line, but defending was the last thing on his mind as he launched his career in claret and blue. I chatted with him the day before his debut and he told me how he would dearly love to emulate the feat of one of his boyhood heroes, Cyrille Regis, by scoring in his first game for Villa.

Regis had done it in a 3-2 win at Sheffield Wednesday on the opening day of the 1991-92 campaign. Dublin could hardly have imagined, as he revealed his debut-day wish, that he would also score in a 3-2 win. Not that it was an exact repetition of Regis's feat. Dion did it against Tottenham Hotspur in a home match – and he didn't settle for just one.

Better still, his two goals were both scored in front of the Holte End, and you wouldn't have found a single home supporter who was concerned in the slightest that both came gift-wrapped as the result of some haphazard Spurs defending. Just over half-an-hour had elapsed when Alan Wright's corner created total panic among the visitors, leaving the new striker a simple task of firing home unchallenged from close range. Four minutes later, Darren Anderton and John Scales inexplicably left the ball to each other and it rolled to Dublin, who was only too grateful to slot a low shot past stranded goalkeeper Espen Baardsen.

The new boy had the ball in the net for a third time, too, only to be frustrated by an offside decision. His first Villa hat-trick would have to wait – but only for one week. Seven days later, Gregory's boys made club history by extending their unbeaten start to 12 matches with an emphatic 4-1 success at Southampton, and there was no question about the hero of the hour.

This time, Dublin needed just two minutes to open his account, meeting Steve Watson's right-wing centre with a perfectly-placed header which left Saints keeper Paul Jones helpless. Matthew Le Tissier, a player who was so often a thorn in Villa's side, equalised early in the second half but within three minutes, Dublin sent a 25-yard shot curling just inside the left-hand post. Paul Merson made it 3-1 and then, with five minutes remaining, Dublin flicked home the fourth with the outside of his right boot.

It was party time at The Dell, and even though the team's run was brought to an end by Liverpool at Villa Park the following Saturday, both goals in a 4-2 setback were scored by the deadly Dion, taking his haul to seven in three games. That incredible ratio deservedly earned him the Premiership Player of the Month award for November, as well as an England call-up for the friendly against the Czech Republic at Wembley, where he laid on the second goal for club colleague Paul Merson in a 2-0 win.

But surely his amazing form couldn't continue? Of course it couldn't. As if to underline the fact he is only human, Dublin missed a glorious chance to secure victory in the dying seconds of a 2-2 draw at Nottingham Forest and subsequently drew blanks in a home draw against Manchester United and a 2-1 defeat at Chelsea.

The midweek reversal at Stamford Bridge, Villa's first Premiership away defeat since Gregory's appointment as manager 10 months earlier, prompted doubts that the team were starting to lose their way, despite remaining at the top of the table. There were also concerns that Dublin wasn't quite as lethal as early indications had led us to believe. Both notions were blown away in an incredible match four days later. Trailing to two Dennis Bergkamp goals at half-time, there seemed to be no way back against an Arsenal side who had conceded only seven goals in 16 matches. But after Julian Joachim had reduced the deficit just past the hour mark, the Holte's new hero took centre stage, equalising when he diverted Alan Thompson's cross-shot past David Seaman and then grabbing the winner seven minutes from time.

Villa, dislodged by Manchester United 24 hours earlier after 13 weeks at the top, were back in pole position, where they remained until early in the New Year. Unfortunately for Dublin, the honeymoon period was over. Troubled by a hernia problem, he played only twice in January and it was February before his next goal came along, a consolation penalty on the day Villa were humiliated 4-1 at home by his former club Coventry City. After that, he was on target only once until the end of the season, in a 3-0 romp against Southampton, but his willingness to play through the pain barrier sent his stock soaring, not least with his manager.

"Dion has a heart the size of a bucket," said Gregory. "He is desperate to play. Even at 70 to 80 per cent of full throttle, he is still a handful for teams. Most people suffering the way he is wouldn't even be putting the shirt on but Dion is a totally dedicated professional and hates missing games. He's got the first and most important attribute that all footballers must have – application."

He finally called time on his debut Villa campaign 15 minutes from the end of a 2-1 defeat by Manchester United at Old Trafford on the first Saturday of May, a knee problem forcing him to miss the final two matches against Charlton and Arsenal. If we were impressed by his bravery in playing for so long in such discomfort, though, we had seen nothing yet.

The misfortune he suffered the following December would have been the end of the road for many footballers, but not Dion Dublin. Three months after suffering the injury which could have left him paralysed, he was back in action, scoring the crucial penalty which took Villa to the FA Cup final.

But let's not race too far ahead in the story. Ask any Villa supporter to recall their most vivid memory of Dion and it will almost certainly be the blistering start to his time with the club or the horrific neck injury from which he made a remarkable recovery. Yet during those dark days at the end of one century and the start of another, he was actually on course to beat Peter Withe's total of 20 goals in one season, a figure which has not been bettered since Withe achieved the feat in the League Championship campaign of 1980-81.

As if to atone for the injury frustrations of the previous few months, he started the 1999-00 season with a thumping volley in the opening home match victory over Everton before netting twice in a 2-2 draw with West Ham five days later. Then there were winning goals against both Middlesbrough and Bradford City. By mid-December, he had scored 12 times in 21 league and cup games, which would have become 13 in 22 if the League Cup quarter-final against the Hammers had not been declared void after the London club fielded an ineligible player.

Of those dozen goals, nine had been scored in 17 Premiership matches. At the rate of one every two games, he was well on track to pass Withe's total but fate was about to alter his season in the cruellest and most dramatic fashion.

Three days after the "game that never was" at Upton Park, Villa beat Sheffield Wednesday 2-1 at home but it was the worst afternoon of Dublin's life – and not because he had a penalty saved by Pavel Srnicek. Five minutes from time, he accidentally collided with Wednesday substitute Gerald Sibon on the halfway line and although he managed to walk to the touchline with physio Jim Walker, it was evident something was amiss. Although Dublin insisted he wanted to go back on to the pitch, it was clearly out of the question.

Eventually he was carefully placed on a stretcher and transferred to the medical room and then to hospital where he underwent a four-hour operation on a crushed vertebra. It emerged later that only Walker's prompt action in protecting the spinal cord from damage prevented the possibility of him being paralysed.

The physio even sat in on the operation, something he had been requested to do on other occasions by players who were nervous about going under the knife but who had been comforted by his presence as they were anaesthetised. This time, though, even the experienced Walker admitted to being "gobsmacked" by the complexity of the surgery which was carried out on the club's top marksman, and manager Gregory was shaken by the serious consequences of what had seemed a harmless collision.

"It's been said that football is more important than life, but something like this puts that statement in perspective," commented the Villa boss. "There are certain things which are far more important than being able to kick a bag of wind around. It's a major blow losing Dion but it hardly compares to the stark reality that he could have been in a wheelchair. That's how bad the injury was."

Bad as it was, it wasn't about to prevent Dublin from amazing us all once again, this time with his remarkable healing powers. Three months and one week later he stepped back on to the Villa Park pitch as an 80th minute substitute for Italian Benito Carbone in a 2-0 win over Derby County and during the final 10 minutes of that match he did enough to prove he was ready for consideration for the FA Cup semi-final against Bolton Wanderers.

He had been to Wembley twice while with Manchester United but had done no more than watch from the stands in his 'civvies' without, as he put it, "earning the right to play." This time, he was determined to be involved, if not from the outset, then definitely from the subs' bench. That was how the semi-final scenario unfolded. For nearly 70 minutes of a truly dreadful game, he watched from the bench before taking over from Carbone for the final 20 minutes plus half-an-hour of extra time which was equally unproductive. It was a stodgy, tedious contest, no question about that, although Villa must have started to believe they were destined for the final when Dean Holdsworth missed a glorious chance during the additional 30 minutes.

In the end, it came down to a penalty shoot-out, and while Villa's record in these tension-charged showdowns has been largely unimpressive down the years, at least this one went their way. Steve Stone scored from the first spot-kick and Holdsworth from the second to suggest it was going to be tight. But after Lee Hendrie had converted Villa's second penalty, David James saved from Allan Johnston – and then repeated the feat from Michael Johansen after Gareth Barry had taken the score to 3-1.

Next up was Dublin. If he scored, Villa were through to the club's first FA Cup final for 43 years. He did, driving firmly past goalkeeper Jussi Jaaskelainen before being mobbed by his delighted team-mates. Not that Dion had ever been worried about the outcome. Before the match he had told Gregory he would go on and score the winner. First we had admired his powers of recovery, now it seemed he had psychic powers, too.

By the end of the season he had also consolidated his position as Villa's leading scorer, taking his goal haul to 15 in all competitions – not bad for someone who had been sidelined for more than three months. More importantly, his second in a 4-2 win at Tottenham conclusively proved he was no longer even thinking about his neck. It was a goal which was as brave as it was beautiful as he leapt into the air to convert Carbone's centre with a superb overhead kick for the equaliser after Spurs had led 2-0. Villa supporters' hearts were in their mouths as he landed awkwardly but he was up and about his business in no time at all. Within a minute, he had headed down a long kick from James for Carbone to fire the visitors ahead.

Unfortunately, the memorable victory at White Hart Lane

proved to be Villa's last of the season. For once, Dublin failed to amaze us on FA Cup final day. He conjured up nothing special, Villa were unadventurous in the extreme and Chelsea won 1-0 in the last final to be played beneath Wembley's famous twin towers.

As the bulldozers moved in to demolish the famous old stadium that winter, Dublin was also left feeling decidedly flat. Villa's final position of eighth in 2000-01 was respectable enough, but they were left to reflect on how much better it might have been with a better return from their main striker. True, Dion was the club's leading scorer, but his total of nine goals – eight in the league plus one against Marila Pribram in the Intertoto Cup – was hardly an achievement to shout from the rooftops.

Needless to say, there were suggestions that his neck injury had robbed him of his cutting edge but a more likely explanation is that he suffered the sort of slump which afflicts most players throughout the course of their careers. Certainly, the theory that his enthusiasm had dwindled because of an over-cautious approach was dispelled in September, when he witnessed at close hand the double leg fracture which ended the career of Belgian striker Luc Nilis.

The sight of Nilis's horrific collision with Ipswich goalkeeper Richard Wright was a sickening experience for all of Villa's players but Dublin, as professional as ever, got on with the job in hand and headed the second goal in a 2-1 victory at Portman Road. He also rammed home a penalty against Bradford City the following week, and was adamant that his early-season goal drought had nothing to do with his serious injury the previous season. "It hasn't been on my mind," he insisted. "I haven't thought about it at all. If you do that you start going backwards."

He also stressed how hard goals are to come by in the Premiership and his modest output underlined the point. It hardly helped that he had been robbed of a potentially lethal strike partner and he was even substituted in consecutive games against Arsenal and Sunderland. Yet the man who brought him off, manager John Gregory, admitted he still had immense faith in Dublin, who finally got back on the score sheet in late November with a goal to savour, a predatory close-range finish to open the scoring against his former club Coventry.

It was after the 1-1 draw at Highfield Road that Gregory claimed part of Dublin's problem was that his place was never under threat. All managers liked competition for places, he said, and Dion didn't have anyone making him look over his shoulder. For all that, the manager had nothing but praise for his striker's attitude during his lean spell. "Deep down, he has been concerned, as all goalscorers are when they are not scoring," said Gregory. "Dion has been aware of his responsibilities but he hasn't allowed it to get to him. The usual thing for strikers in this position is to blame the service they are getting but he has never done that."

The goal against the Sky Blues did wonders for Dion's self-belief – initially, at least. Seven days later, he headed in a David Ginola cross after just four minutes of the home game against Newcastle United and two weeks further down the line he was on target with a glancing header in a 2-2 draw against Manchester City at Villa Park.

While that was something of an early Christmas present, it proved to be a bleak midwinter for the second year running. There was no broken neck to worry about this time, more like a broken spirit as he went three-and-a-half months without scoring. It was the return game against City at Maine Road at the end of March before he hit the target again in a 3-1 win. How grateful he must have been that goalkeeper Nicky Weaver decided to prove he was also adept as an outfield player as the seconds ticked down to half-time. Rather than taking the safety-first option of a booted clearance from Spencer Prior's back pass, Weaver attempted to dribble the ball around Dublin and ended up on his backside as he slipped in the wet, treacherous conditions. Dion needed no second invitation to end his drought by stroking the ball into an unguarded net to put Villa 2-1 ahead at the interval.

Not that he received any credit from his manager. Gregory was already in the dressing room, preparing his half-time pep talk, and spent 10 minutes telling his players they needed a second goal, before goalkeeper Peter Enckelman whispered in his ear that Dion had already scored it!

Not for the first time, one Dublin goal led to another. Four nights later, Villa beat Leicester City for the first time since February 1988, and Dion once again capitalised on goalkeeping generosity to score against his hometown club. This time his header was grasped under the bar by Simon Royce, who was adjudged by a linesman to have carried the ball over the line. The visitors, who had taken the lead a few minutes earlier, were incensed and even John Gregory admitted he couldn't believe the linesman had been able to see clearly whether the ball had gone in or not. Gregory wasn't complaining, though, and neither was Dublin. Nor was midfielder Lee Hendrie, whose stunning 72nd-minute strike ensured that the misery inflicted by the Foxes on the Villans was over at long last.

Ten days later, Dion was on target again, firing home Villa's fastest goal of the season after just 75 seconds of a 2-1 home win over Everton. It was sheer quality, too. Ian Taylor cleverly stepped over Alan Wright's low centre and Dublin wrong-footed David Weir before sending his shot past goalkeeper Paul Gerrard.

That strike illustrated what a clinical finisher he still was, but there was precious little opportunity for him to display his predatory talents in 2001-02, when his starting appearances in league games didn't even reach double figures as he was kept on the sidelines for long periods by the Darius Vassell-Juan Pablo Angel partnership. An Intertoto Cup semi-final winner against French club Rennes suggested we may see Dublin back to his prolific best, but it wasn't to be. Gregory preferred, for the most part, to have the younger duo of Vassell and Angel up front.

For all that, there were still trademark headed goals against Liverpool, West Ham and Arsenal to savour, and Dublin was at pains to stress that he wasn't looking to get away because of his limited activity. "I signed a long deal when I moved here from Coventry," he stressed, "and I have no intention of going anywhere else."

As well as being a consummate professional, he also made his mark off the pitch as an ambassador for the *Prince's Trust* charity. In November, he joined chairman Doug Ellis and the club's other directors in welcoming Prince Charles when the prince officially opened the new Trinity Road Stand. He was perfectly at ease in the presence of royalty, answering the Prince's questions about where Villa stood in the table (third at the time) and who they were due to play next (Middlesbrough). For his part, the Prince passed on best wishes from his son Prince William, who had delighted everyone down Witton way by declaring himself to be a Villa supporter.

Rubbing shoulders with royalty wasn't about to make Dion any more of a regular in the Villa line-up, however, and later in the season he was loaned out to Millwall, who were chasing promotion to the Premiership. It wasn't exactly the most appealing of moves for a player of his stature but, typically, he applied himself to his task at the New Den, helping the south London club to the play-offs where they lost on aggregate to Birmingham City in the semi-finals, despite his fine headed goal at St. Andrew's in the first leg. Even though he wasn't wearing claret and blue at the time, that was a moment for Villa fans to cherish, and there was another one on the final day. Millwall's failure to reach the play-off final effectively brought his loan spell to an end and he was back on Villa's substitutes' bench for the last match of the season against Chelsea. For 84 minutes he was no more than a spectator at Stamford Bridge, but then he replaced Darius Vassell – and within four minutes he had headed the third goal in a 3-1 win. Even in a largely disappointing season, Dublin managed to have the final word.

Had Millwall been promoted, the chances are his move would have become permanent. In the event, he remained in the Midlands and proved he still had plenty to offer Villa. The 2002-03 season was, up to that point, the club's least successful since the advent of the Premier League and the threat of relegation was only removed by victory over Sunderland on the penultimate weekend. Dion, though, had plenty of cause for personal satisfaction as he made 35 league and cup appearances and scored 15 goals, a figure which equalled his best return in a Villa shirt.

Not that there was any indication of such a valuable contribution during the first few weeks. With numerous Villa players still on holiday following the World Cup finals in South Korea and Japan, he played centre-back in the opening Intertoto Cup fixture in Zurich and was, indeed, appointed captain in the absence of Olof Mellberg and Steve Staunton. But he didn't even make the subs' bench for the first five Premiership matches and must have begun to wonder if his days as a Villa man were coming to an end.

Thankfully, help was at hand in the form of reserve coach Kevin MacDonald. High-profile players often find difficulty in getting motivated for second-team games in front of a couple of hundred spectators, but MacDonald discouraged any notion of a negative approach.

"Kevin makes you believe you are going to get back in the first team," said Dublin at the time. "He both praises you and lets you know if you are not doing very well. That's what you need when you are in the reserves. He's very positive – one of the best coaches I've worked with."

MacDonald's method was to pay dividends, too. Dublin was re-introduced to first-team action when he went on as a second-half substitute in the Second City derby against Blues at St. Andrew's. He could do nothing to prevent a humiliating 3-0 defeat at the hands of the old enemy, but his performance at least ensured his return to the squad on a regular basis. Sub again against Everton in the next match, he replaced Peter Crouch in the 81st minute and scored four minutes later to clinch a 3-2 success. Then he netted twice in a 3-0 League Cup defeat of Luton Town. From a season which had seemed to be going nowhere, he was suddenly Villa's leading scorer with an admittedly modest total of three goals.

Skipper Mellberg was among those to sing his praises for the way he had battled his way back into contention, insisting that throughout his absence from the first team, Dublin had worked as hard as ever in training. The Swedish international also revealed that Dion's influence was not restricted to his impact on the pitch.

"He is always in a good mood and is a nice guy to have in the dressing room," said Mellberg. "He's a good player, very strong with a good ability to head the ball. He has proved how important he can be with his goalscoring ability." Dublin's striking partner Darius Vassell was another player with nothing but praise, describing him as "a big brother."

"Dion has been tremendous towards me," added Vassell. "He's like a second captain and he's always helping me. He is always lifting me and keeping me going at 100 per cent, regardless of how he is playing himself. I will always be thankful to him for that."

And young striker Stefan Moore, who had broken into the side earlier that season, also expressed his gratitude to DD. "When I made my debut, Dion didn't stop talking to me," said Moore. "He is a major influence. He never stops telling me about the things I'm doing right and the things I have to improve on. It was inspiring to have someone with his experience alongside me. His influence is something I will never forget."

Even after his departure, he continued to be appreciated. Just listen to Stefan's younger brother Luke, who made his Villa first-team debut a few months before Dublin left:

"Dion always used to tell me to be prepared for when my chance came along and I took his advice. I learned a lot from Dion and I think a lot of the boys missed having him around after he had gone. I certainly missed him. When it came to giving good advice, he was priceless."

It was easy to see why Dion's team-mates had so much time for him.

A penalty miss in a goalless derby against West Bromwich Albion at The Hawthorns in November was a moment to forget, but the following week he reached a personal milestone when he scored his 100th Premiership goal in a 4-1 thrashing of West Ham – and that launched an impressive spell of 10 goals in 15 games. There was no mid-winter depression for Dion Dublin this time around.

His goals couldn't prevent a dramatic 4-3 League Cup quarter-final defeat by Liverpool or a shock 4-1 reversal at the hands of a Dwight Yorke-inspired Blackburn Rovers in the third round of the FA Cup, but ultimately they played a crucial role in Villa maintaining top-flight status. His fine run also included two against Blackburn as revenge was taken for the Cup exit in a 3-0 league win in March, although he then missed a defeat by the same margin at Charlton through suspension – and he quickly ensured he would have to sit out three more games.

Exactly what made him head-butt Robbie Savage in the return Second City derby at Villa Park we will possibly never know. Clearly, a derogatory remark was made by the Birmingham City midfielder to prompt such a violent reaction, which left referee Mark Halsey with no option but to send him off. Dublin wasn't revealing anything, but he moved quickly to apologise for his uncharacteristic action.

After a sleepless night, during which he admonished himself over and over for acting so recklessly, he called a meeting of Villa's players in order to say sorry to them face-to-face for letting them down. With Icelandic midfielder Joey Gudjonsson also being sent off, it was no great surprise that nine-man Villa had lost 2-0.

Dublin also faced the media in an attempt to explain why he had lost his composure, although he insisted that Savage's remark had not been racist. "What was said is irrelevant," he told reporters. "My actions were wrong. It was the wrong reaction and I'm ashamed of what I have done. I have let down the players, the manager and the staff and, most importantly, I have let myself down."

While his assault on Savage could hardly be condoned (although some diehard Villa fans might just disagree), his humble reaction to the unsavoury incident earned him plenty of admirers, not least manager Graham Taylor, who was totally flabbergasted by what had taken place.

"I have a great deal of respect for Dion and I've said many times I have admired his professional approach," said Taylor. "If I had picked anyone, I would never have picked Dion to do that. He will not be able to explain what happened to anybody – he will not be able to explain it to himself."

As Villa limped towards the finishing line and a final position of 16th, Dublin signed off with one more goal, a header after going on as a substitute in a 1-1 draw at Newcastle, before his future again became a subject for conjecture that summer. With Taylor gone, he certainly seemed to have no great part in new manager David O'Leary's plans and there was talk of a loan transfer to Rotherham United. Just like his predecessors in the hot seat though, the new boss soon discovered Dion's value to the team.

He saw barely 20 minutes of action in the first half-dozen

games and with Darius Vassell, Marcus Allback and Juan Pablo Angel ahead of him in the pecking order, there was little prospect of more regular involvement, even after Peter Crouch was packed off to Norwich City on a three-month loan.

But O'Leary had clearly taken note of John Gregory's prediction five years earlier that when Dublin was no longer playing centre-forward he could switch to centre-half. When regular centre-backs Olof Mellberg and Ronny Johnsen were both ruled out of a League Cup tie at Wycombe, Dublin and full-back Mark Delaney slotted in effortlessly at the heart of the defence. All right, so they weren't unduly inconvenienced by their League Two opponents during a 5-0 stroll at the Causeway Stadium, but Dublin proved at Stamford Bridge four days later that Gregory had known exactly what he was talking about.

Paired alongside Turkish international Alpay Ozalan on this occasion, he produced a fine performance to subdue Chelsea striker Jimmy-Floyd Hasselbaink. True, Hasselbaink scored the game's only goal two minutes before half-time, but even the Londoners' manager Claudio Ranieri admitted afterwards that his expensively-assembled team had been lucky to hold on for all three points.

With Mellberg fit again, Dion was back to his familiar role of an unused substitute for the next two games, but another call to defensive duty was just around the corner. When Johnsen was ruled out of the home match against Everton, he stepped in alongside Mellberg, marked Wayne Rooney out of the game and was given glowing media reviews. Matthew Syed of *The Times* gave him a mark of nine out of ten; Hyder Jawad, naming him Villa's Man of the Match, observed in the *Birmingham Post* that Dublin 'marked Wayne Rooney with so much composure that it was not easy to know which one was the England international.'

If it was something of a bonus that a striker should be performing so well at the back at this advanced stage of his career, there was an even bigger treat in store. Never mind his defensive qualities, Dublin also pushed forward into more familiar territory whenever the opportunity arose – and proved that he still had an eye for goal.

A header against Newcastle United earned a draw at St. James's Park for the second time in little more than six months, and then he had the audacity to score the winner at home to Southampton with a spectacular overhead kick. Not that he wasn't gainfully employed for the other 89 minutes of those two matches. On Tyneside, he subdued Alan Shearer; at Villa Park, he nullified the twin threat of James Beattie and Kevin Phillips.

Yet just as we were poised to herald a Dublin Renaissance, it became increasingly evident that his days at Villa Park were drawing to a close. He once again got forward from a defensive role to score in a 5-0 romp against his hometown club Leicester City at the Walkers Stadium, but a home win over Leeds United on the first Saturday in February proved to be his last starting appearance in claret and blue. The remainder of his season comprised half-a-dozen walk-on parts, four views from the bench and four days off.

But surely such an eventful Villa career couldn't end with a whimper? Of course it couldn't. After his cameo appearance in the final game against United and the subsequent lap of honour, he found himself back out on the pitch for a lingering farewell.

"It was an emotional time," he said afterwards. "There were 15,000 people out there and I was pushed out to say goodbye on my own. You grow close to the fans. They have been good to me. I've had some bad times when I haven't been scoring, but they stuck by me. But it's over now. It hit me when I went out on to the pitch after everyone else had gone. That was when it sank in."

The Dublin days were, indeed, all over. But the memories live on.

DION DUBLIN - CAREER STATS

BORN:	Leicester
DATE OF BIRTH:	April 22 1969
JOINED VILLA:	November 1998
VILLA LEAGUE APPS:	155
GOALS:	48
VILLA CUP APPS:	34
GOALS	11
INT. CAPS (England):	4
GOALS:	0

1997-
Gareth
Barry

"From the coolest teenager on the planet to a fully matured leader of men…" If you're looking for a definitive description of Gareth Barry, you won't find a more succinct appraisal than that provided by a lifelong Villa supporter. Richard Whitehead balances his opinion by pointing out that Barry may not have quite fulfilled the extraordinary potential he showed as a 17-year-old, when he was frequently compared to Bobby Moore. But, as Richard also observes, Gareth has nevertheless evolved into a bona fide Villa legend – wearing the No. 6 shirt made famous by European Cup-winning skipper Dennis Mortimer.

Yet sometimes you look at Barry and think the statistics must be lying. There are times when he looks no more than a slip of a lad, which in some ways he isn't. It's just that he has performed so consistently in the Premiership for almost a decade, whether he has been required in central defence, in midfield or at left-back, that you get the feeling he should really look older than his 26 years.

It's difficult to comprehend that this quietly-spoken young man – not nearly as painfully shy as he once was, but still reserved and unassuming – had made 352 appearances for Aston Villa by the end of the 2006-07 season.

Only 16 players have represented the club more often, and while he faces a long haul to match Charlie Aitken's record total of 660 appearances, it's not difficult to envisage him joining Gordon Cowans and Billy Walker as one of those who have clocked up more than 500 games in a Villa shirt.

Football can be unpredictable but all the indications are that Barry, sleek, stylish and one of the Premiership's best, will be plying his trade in claret and blue for the foreseeable future. True, he expressed the view during the summer of 2006 that his career may be better served elsewhere, but the arrival of Martin O'Neill as manager prompted him to re-evaluate his situation.

O'Neill, feeling his way into his new job, asked Barry to do him a favour by at least sticking around until Christmas before making a decision. Barry agreed – and then changed his mind. No, he wasn't going to wait until the festive season. He had seen enough of O'Neill, assistant manager John Robertson and coach Steve Walford, to commit his future to the club there and then. Once the terms of the agreement had been sorted out, he signed a new four-year contract on the morning of Villa's home match against Newcastle United at the end of August.

The news, announced to supporters just before kick-off that Sunday afternoon, was greeted with tumultuous applause, which was hardly surprising. Hugely popular from the day he made his first-team debut as a slender teenager, he had grown to be regarded as one of the club's all-time greats. The fans were understandably delighted he was staying.

A week earlier, his already immense stature at Villa Park had gone up another notch when O'Neill had appointed him club captain ahead of the opening-day match against Arsenal.

"It was a great honour to be named club captain," says Gareth. "I'd captained the team on quite a few occasions when Olof Mellberg had been injured or suspended but it was great to be handed the captaincy for the season. I'd begun to wonder if it might happen when I was captain in one or two pre-season games. To be given the armband to lead out the team at the Emirates Stadium was a wonderful feeling."

By the end of the campaign, he had achieved a couple of other notable feats. Not only did he become Villa's highest Premiership appearance-maker with 290 games – 30 more than previous record holder Alan Wright – he also joined an elite group of just 13 players who have converted 10 or more penalties for the club. One of Gareth Barry's best school subjects was maths but he surely couldn't have envisaged, sitting at his desk 10 years earlier, that he would go on to conjure up such an impressive set of figures.

Born in the seaside resort of Hastings, Barry looked destined to play for his local club Brighton & Hove Albion when he progressed through the Seagulls' schoolboy ranks. But his potential had not gone unnoticed in other parts of the country and in July 1997 he opted to leave the south-coast club and join Villa's Academy.

"It was my last year at school and Brighton had offered me a two-year YTS contract," he recalls. "But other clubs were showing an interest in me. One of Villa's scouts had come down to a few games and then he brought Bryan Jones (Villa's Academy Director) to have a look at me.

"They invited me for a one-week trial around March-April time and I trained with the youth team as well as playing for about an hour of a friendly against VS Rugby. After that, Bryan said the club were offering me a YTS contract. I had a choice between Villa, Arsenal, Chelsea and Crystal Palace, or I could have stayed at Brighton. But I really liked it here. Some people saw it as strange decision, with London only 70 or 80 minutes from where I lived, but I didn't really fancy living in London."

In his first season in claret and blue, Gareth was a regular in the youth side, helping them to victory in the Midland Youth Cup, and such was his progress that he also made seven appearances for the reserves.

"The more I trained, the more I grew in confidence," he says. "I enjoyed the day-to-day banter with the other lads and my game seemed to improve with every training session. The youth-team coaches had a good reputation of bringing players through and every time I trained I got better. It also helped that a lad called Michael Standing had joined from Brighton at the same time. It was good to have someone around who I knew. We spent almost every minute of the day together."

Better still, he signed a professional contract when he turned 17 in February 1998 – ironically on the day Brian Little resigned as manager – and barely a month later he sampled the atmosphere of Premiership football for the first time, travelling with the first team to a game against Wimbledon at Selhurst Park, where new manager John Gregory insisted that he should change into kit and warm up with the other players.

He was then named as a substitute for the home match against West Ham and although he remained on the bench that afternoon, it became clear just how highly he was regarded when he was again among the subs for the penultimate match of the season against Sheffield Wednesday at Hillsborough.

When Ian Taylor was forced out of the action by injury just after half-time, the manager had no hesitation in handing Barry his first-team debut and the youngster blended in effortlessly. Perhaps it helped that Villa were two-up by the time he went on, but he looked born to the part as Villa played the Owls off the park to record a 3-1 win. If his outward demeanour was one of serenity, though, he certainly didn't feel that way.

"Whenever people ask about my most nervous moment, I always think back to that day," he says. "My nerves were really jangling when I went on because I'd never experienced playing in front of big crowds, with big points at stake. Then there was the thought that the whole country would be watching on *Match of the Day* that night. That was the first time my nerves really got the better of me."

Eight days later, with Villa needing to beat Arsenal at home in order to have a chance of European qualification, he was given his full debut. It was a bold decision by Gregory against an Arsenal side who had already been crowned champions and would later complete a Double by winning the FA Cup. But the manager had as much faith in Barry's temperament as he did in his ability. If there were any fears the occasion would be too much for him, the youngster dispelled them from the outset. Rather than looking what he was – Villa's youth-team captain – he gave off the aura of a man among men, trading tackles with the likes of Patrick Vieira, winning his fair share of them, and using the ball intelligently.

He also gave us our first glimpse of his versatility that day. When Ugo Ehiogu was sent off for a second booking and Villa were reduced to 10 men, Barry was switched to a central defensive role alongside Gareth Southgate – and looked as comfortable against the twin threat of Ian Wright and Nicolas Anelka as he had in midfield. Even with the disadvantage of being a man short, Villa signed off the season with a 1-0 win and Barry played as big a part as anyone.

He had been looking forward to the summer but suddenly he didn't want the season to end. Even so, he could hardly have imagined that his days as a second-team player were effectively over after barely a handful of matches. In his mind, he had been given a nice little taste of top-level football. Now he was ready to buckle down and continue his football education with an extended run in the reserves or a place on the first-team bench.

But as the 1998-99 campaign dawned, suspensions to two players resulted in him being plunged into the pressure cooker atmosphere of Villa's Premiership opener at Everton.

Steve Staunton had returned to Liverpool during the close season, while summer signing David Unsworth would also soon be heading home to Merseyside after his infamous U-turn. Having arrived from West Ham, Unsworth was at Villa for only a matter of days before deciding he had made a mistake; that he would really prefer to rejoin Everton, the club where he had started his career.

As it was, Unsworth was still a Villa player as the season got under way but both he and Ugo Ehiogu were suspended so Gregory was stretched to the limit defensively. The manager's solution was to introduce Gareth Barry into a back three alongside Riccardo Scimeca and Gareth Southgate – and once again the youngster responded positively to a daunting challenge.

His calm, assured performance at Goodison Park was enough to persuade the Villa boss that Unsworth's impending departure was no great inconvenience after all. In Barry, he had a perfect replacement without having to venture back into the transfer market, and the outstanding teenager remained an ever-present throughout Villa's history-making 12-match unbeaten start to a league campaign. For all that, he kept his feet firmly on the floor, a fact acknowledged and appreciated by his manager. "I've seen so many players destroyed by putting them on a pedestal at 17," said Gregory at the time. "You sometimes don't hear of them at 19 but Gareth is more down to earth. He can be anything. We will be the ones to blame if he doesn't succeed, because there's plenty to work with. He's young, fit and hungry. He's a quick learner and has a lot of talent."

As for the young man himself, he could barely believe what was happening. His two games the previous season had both resulted in wins, now the team were unbeaten in another 12 league matches. "I started thinking: 'We're going to win the league here', because I didn't know anything different. I was in the team and we were winning games. If I'm honest, I probably got a bit carried away with it all.

"Sometimes I had to pinch myself to realise it was really happening. I could have been sitting behind a desk at school because if I hadn't made the grade I would have stayed on in the sixth form. Instead I was playing against people like Alan Shearer. But more experienced players like Gareth Southgate warned me it wouldn't always be like this and as the season went on our results started to sway a bit."

All the same, Gareth was undeniably on the fast track to the top. He made more than 30 first-team appearances during that first full season, as well as being capped three times by England U21s and being invited to train with Glenn Hoddle's full national squad. He also signed a new five-year contract on turning 18 – a massive vote of confidence for someone who had made just 14 full Premiership appearances – and it was no surprise when he was voted Villa's Young Player of the Year.

There were a couple of late-season goals to savour, too. His first, after he had gone on as a second-half substitute for Dion Dublin, sealed a 2-0 victory which condemned a Nottingham Forest side managed by former Villa boss Ron Atkinson to relegation. His second was part of a bizarre scenario against another relegation-threatened team, Charlton Athletic, in the final home match of the season.

Amazingly, Barry was on target twice in the opening seven minutes – once at each end. In the third minute, he was pressurised into heading an own goal past Michael Oakes but four minutes later he redeemed himself by volleying the equaliser. Charlton won 4-3, although it was no more than a stay of execution for the London club, whose demotion was merely delayed by a week.

"That was a strange sort of game, particularly the start," he says. "The ball came in from a corner, skewed off my head the wrong way and went in. Straight away, I was thinking I had to try and do something to make up for it. Thankfully I volleyed into an open net a few minutes later and that calmed me down."

Although Barry was now making his name as a defender, there was invariably an aura of elegance to his play. At times he created problems for himself and fellow defenders by trying to be constructive, when an unattractive boot into the stand might have been more effective. But if his leaning towards brain rather than brawn occasionally set Villa nerves on edge in those early days, his manager wasn't about to try to change him.

"If he wants to bring the ball down in our penalty area I won't knock it out of him, I will encourage it," said Gregory. "Maybe there's hope for English football after all. When you consider how we lost Steve Staunton and then couldn't persuade David Unsworth to stay, Gareth's emergence to fill the same position is like a gift from the gods."

Gregory also described the rapidly-emerging young defender as "a phenomenon" although not everyone was quite as enamoured with the young man's rapid progress. Miffed that such a talented footballer had been whisked away from under their noses after playing nearly 100 games for them from U11 to U16 level, Brighton had, earlier in the season, vigorously sought redress for their loss.

The Seagulls argued that they should be compensated for the money they had invested in his career and a Football League appeals committee agreed. Villa were ordered to pay £150,000 with various clauses added on – £200,000 after 20 senior games, £200,000 after 40 and £250,000 after 60, plus £25,000 for an U21 cap and £200,000 for an England cap. It all added up to just over £1m, which seemed a lot of money then but subsequently amounted to peanuts. Not that the club were too happy with the ruling. After paying the initial £150,000, they refused to hand over the first appearance-related instalment, claiming Barry was over-priced and demanding the tribunal reveal the reasons behind their figures.

The matter was eventually dealt with by the Premier League Board, who ensured that the money, plus interest, was paid. But there was clearly a fair amount of animosity between the clubs. Villa felt Brighton had been over-compensated, and Gregory claimed that their chairman Dick Knight wouldn't recognise Barry even if "he stood on Brighton beach in an Albion shirt with a ball tucked under his arm and a seagull on his head." This was possibly true, but Knight would have been fully aware of the departure of Barry and his pal Michael Standing to Villa Park. The Brighton chairman was Standing's uncle!

While Gregory's seaside analogy raised a chuckle or two, Barry didn't have to go to such lengths as standing on a beach with a seagull perched on him. He was earning plenty of recognition in the Midlands – and beyond. The following season, Villa found themselves dipping in their pockets yet again as he reached 40 appearances, then 60, before making his full England debut in a friendly against Ukraine at Wembley in May.

It wasn't his first visit to the famous old stadium that spring. He had also scored one of the penalties in the FA Cup semi-final shoot-out against Bolton as Villa reached the final for the first time since 1957, and while the big day itself was a massive anti-climax, the 1-0 defeat by Chelsea provided Barry with another important learning curve on football's greatest stage.

"Before the Bolton game, I'd never been to Wembley, even to watch a game," he says. "To find myself playing there in an FA Cup semi-final was an overwhelming experience. There was also a lot of pressure on us because we were playing a team from a lower division. Taking that penalty was another nervous moment for me at a young age, but I'm sure it was something which held me in good stead for later. It was a good feeling when the ball hit the net!

"I also have a lot of memories of the final. The atmosphere driving to Wembley was incredible as we passed all the Villa and Chelsea fans. It's just a pity the game won't go down as one of the better finals. To lose it was all the more disappointing so the season ended on a slightly sour note."

That may have been so, but the Midland Football Writers' Association were impressed by Barry's poised, relaxed displays throughout the campaign, naming him as their Young Player of the Year. So was Kevin Keegan, who named him in the 22-man England squad for Euro 2000. So was former Arsenal and

England striker Alan Smith, who had become a respected journalist since hanging up his boots. They say the most accurate assessments of footballers are made by people who have played the game, so how about this from Smith in the *Daily Telegraph* after Villa had beaten Leeds United 3-2 in the fifth round of the Cup?

"One of the Villa player's finer attributes is his quality use of possession. He rarely gave the ball away under pressure. In fact it was from his long but accurately-placed free-kick that Benito Carbone scored the first of his three goals.

"One audacious piece of skill drew unanimous applause, Barry reading a through ball and dragging it back through his legs before confidently flicking it away to Alan Wright. Just to show it was no fluke, he pulled off something similar a little later, perceptively reading another pass and back-heeling to George Boateng from the touchline." Alan Smith may have known more about scoring goals than midfield attributes but he was well aware he had witnessed something pretty special.

Barry had to settle for the role of an unused substitute in Holland and Belgium as England made an early exit from the 2000 European Championship, although he did have some competitive European action that summer. Villa had decided to enter the much-maligned Intertoto Cup for the first time as a possible route to a UEFA Cup place, although their new venture hardly turned out as planned. Despite overcoming Czech side Marila Pribram (formerly Dukla Prague) after joining the competition in the third round, they came unstuck at the hands of Celta Vigo in the semi-final, going down 3-1 on aggregate.

The second leg, played at The Hawthorns because the new Trinity Road stand was under construction, disintegrated into farce when Swiss referee Dieter Schoch sent off three players, including Ian Taylor and Alan Thompson, booked eight others and then blew the final whistle several minutes early.

For Barry, though, it was a significant occasion – it was the night he took his first penalty for Villa. Paul Merson had seen a spot-kick saved by Jose Manuel Pinto in the 41st minute, so when Villa were awarded another on the stroke of half-time, Barry stepped forward. The cool manner in which he despatched his kick provided further evidence of maturity beyond his years, although it was to be his only goal of a season in which he experienced the first real setbacks of his career.

Although he made his first starts for the national side against France, Finland and Italy, as well as going on as a substitute against Germany in the last competitive match at the old Wembley Stadium, his international prospects nosedived when Sven Goran Eriksson took over as coach of the national team.

Eriksson's first game in charge was against Spain at Villa Park, which seemed the ideal venue for Barry to show the new England boss what he could do. Instead, his 20th birthday present from the Swede was to be told he wasn't in the squad and that he would be playing for the U21s against their Spanish counterparts at St. Andrew's, 24 hours before the main event.

To his credit, Barry put on a brave face and tried to be philosophical about the situation. Yes, he was disappointed, he admitted, particularly after winning six full caps by his 20th birthday. No, he wouldn't be sulking about his omission. After all, as he pointed out, he could have had a worse start to his career and there was plenty of time ahead of him.

The immediate future, though, was far from bright. Despite a generally composed and assured performance against Derby County at Pride Park the day after his birthday, Barry's clumsy challenge on Deon Burton presented the Rams striker with the opportunity to score the only goal from the penalty spot. Three days later, his slip led to one of Spain's goals as the U21s crashed to a 4-0 defeat.

Sadly, things got worse before they got better. It was bad enough being left out of the England side, but he suddenly found he was no longer an automatic selection for Villa.

Where he had been as comfortable as an old shoe in a three-man central defence, he wasn't regarded by Gregory as such a naturally-gifted left-back or left-sided midfielder in a 4-4-2 formation. As Villa returned to a more conventional line-up, Barry found himself involved less and less – and if he imagined the launch of the following season would bring a change in fortune, he couldn't have been more wrong.

Although he started all six games as Villa won the Intertoto Cup in the summer of 2001, he had to wait until December before making the line-up in the Premiership, and even then it was only because Villa had injury problems. It was a classic case of a highly promising career going into reverse.

"It was a frustrating year because I no longer featured in John Gregory's plans," he says. "He had his own ideas but I think the main thing which affected me was when we changed from 3-5-2 to 4-4-2. I'd been playing left-sided centre-half week in, week out under the old system but once we changed I was in and out for a while and then, suddenly, I wasn't in at all.

"I had been brought up at Villa in that position and I'd played a lot of games there for the first team, but I was also comfortable in other positions. All of my England caps had been at left-back and I was as happy there as in a back three.

"It was strange, really. To have been in the team at such a young age and played a lot of games, it was hard to suddenly be left out. When I look back, maybe I should have reacted differently. As the season went on, John was quoted in the papers, saying I needed to change my game and get my shorts dirtier, which didn't help.

"As I've got older, I realise managers sometimes say these things to try and motivate you. At the time, though, I reacted by saying I wasn't going to change my game. If it happened now, I would think that if it was something which could improve me, I would look at it. But these are the things you learn from."

Nevertheless, it was galling that he should have been left out in the cold, sometimes not even making the subs' bench. Thankfully salvation was just around the corner. By the end of January, Gregory had left and his successor Graham Taylor immediately reinstated Barry to the squad, initially on the bench against Chelsea and then as a regular in midfield for the remaining dozen games of the season.

Even Taylor will acknowledge that his second spell, all 16 months of it, was nowhere near as successful as his first, which had culminated in his appointment as England coach. This time around it ended in ignominious fashion as Villa slumped from eighth in 2002 to 16th a year later. It was an open secret that he simply didn't get on with several of the club's senior players; that his management methods were not in tune with footballers whose huge salaries had, in some cases, removed their hunger and motivation.

But there's no question that GB will be forever grateful to GT for putting him back into forward gear and pointing him towards the role of a middle man. "When Graham took over I was out of the team and my confidence was low," he recalls. "But he showed terrific faith in me and really got my career back on track. At his first training session, he called me over and said there was going to be a fresh start, telling me to re-focus. I never looked back after that.

"You start doubting yourself when you are out of the team for so long. I'd played for England, I'd been to Euro 2000 and I'd played a lot of games for Aston Villa. I kept thinking, I've already done it at the top level but at the same time I started wondering if I might have to drop down a level. So it was perfect when Graham Taylor came in, gave me the right vibes and helped me to get my confidence back."

So impressive was Barry's form on the left of midfield that season, that the club's official website campaigned strongly for his return to the England fold in what had become a problem position for Eriksson. *Left side...right player* was the slogan used by www.avfc.co.uk, and Barry, by then firmly established as captain of the U21s, was flattered that an official club outlet should be backing him for a recall to the full national side.

He could have made no greater claim for a return to the international stage than when Villa drew 1-1 against Manchester United in October. Lining up directly opposite David Beckham, he produced a magnificent display at Old Trafford and there were a couple of occasions when even staunch United fans could only watch in admiration as his trickery had England's golden boy chasing shadows.

Unfortunately, his form had no great effect on the stubborn Swede, Gareth having to settle for a combined total of just 14 minutes action as a substitute against South Africa in May 2003 and Serbia & Montenegro the following month. From a club perspective, though, the important thing was that he was back in the groove in claret and blue, and his more advanced role boosted his goalscoring, too. During the course of the four previous campaigns he had hit the target on just four occasions. In 2002-03, he doubled his haul, scoring in an early season League Cup win at Oxford before surprising everyone – including himself – with three goals in consecutive games against Middlesbrough, Blackburn and Fulham in late January and early February.

He scored four the following season, too, the first of them on a bittersweet opening day at Fratton Park in David O'Leary's first competitive match as manager. Appointed skipper as the new boss surprisingly preferred wayward Turk Alpay Ozalan to Olof Mellberg in central defence, the midfielder converted an 84th-minute penalty in a 2-1 setback by newly-promoted Portsmouth at Fratton Park, only to invite a red card for swearing at a linesman as his frustration at the team's impending defeat boiled over in the dying minutes.

"I was really pumped up for that game," he says. "Our new manager David O'Leary had made me captain and I felt a lot of pressure on my shoulders. We were two-nil down and I'd just won a penalty and scored it, so there was a lot of adrenaline flowing. A few decisions started going against us and I lost my cool. I made a mistake, and I apologised to the manager and the other players after the game. The rule is there that you shouldn't swear at the officials and I hold my hands up – I said something I shouldn't have said to the linesman. I'm sure he had heard worse but some referees let things like that go and others don't. Unfortunately this one didn't. But you learn from things like that. I've been sent off a couple of times since, but for challenges rather than something I said."

His other two league goals, meanwhile, were scored in happier circumstances, helping to ensure victories over Wolves and Middlesbrough, while he also put Villa ahead in a third-round FA Cup tie against United before Sir Alex Ferguson's men hit back to win 2-1. However, even though Villa finished sixth, his own form didn't quite scale the heights of the previous season, when he had been voted the club's Player of the Year. For all that, he still produced some notable performances in central midfield before reverting to his now established role of the left. By then, he had become an integral part of the Villa set-up and it was no surprise when he signed a new four-year contract, describing himself as "part of the Villa family."

Gareth's goalscoring could almost be described as prolific over the course of the next three seasons. Having previously never managed more than four in any given campaign, he netted eight in 2005-06, six in 2006-07 and nine in 2006-07. That was due in part to the fact that he took over as Villa's penalty-taker, although he has also contributed a fair few from open play.

"Since I've played in midfield I don't think my record has been too bad," he insists. "Taking penalties helps but it's good to have your name on the score sheet, no matter how you do it. And it really lifts your confidence when you've just scored a penalty."

His favourite goal to date, though, was the one he scored against his boyhood favourites Tottenham Hotspur in a 1-1 draw at Villa Park in October 2006. With 16 minutes remaining, defeat looked a distinct possibility, Juan Pablo Angel having presented Spurs with an own goal immediately after missing a penalty. Barry assumed the role of penalty-taker after that wayward spot-kick by the Colombian, but his equaliser against the Londoners was from considerably further than 12 yards. Superbly controlling Stiliyan Petrov's pass, he twisted and turned his way past Paul Stalteri and Jermaine Jenas before sending a right foot shot into the far top corner from the left-hand edge of the penalty area.

"A few weeks before, I'd been thinking I hadn't really scored what you could describe as a 'wonder goal' for Villa," he says. "Whether you would put the one against Spurs in that league, I don't know. But I was happy with it!"

Everyone else was, too. It was the front-runner in the club's Goal of the Season contest until the penultimate match, when it was edged out by Patrik Berger's superb effort in the 3-0 victory over Sheffield United. Still, Gareth wasn't complaining at narrowly missing out on that one. At the club's annual awards night, he was deservedly acclaimed Player of the Year.

While Barry can look back at a highly-satisfying Villa career over the best part of a decade, he is also a man who constantly strives for success, both for himself and his team-mates, which is why he seriously considered where his future lay during the summer of 2006. His own form had been consistent throughout David O'Leary's tenancy as manager but over the course of three seasons he had been disillusioned to see Villa slip from sixth, to 10th, to 16th.

"There were no hard feelings between me and David O'Leary but I started to wonder if I needed a fresh start," he admits. "I couldn't see the club moving on to the next level as things were and I felt a change of club might be the best thing for my career.

"There was a fair bit of interest from other clubs, including a couple of firm bids, but Villa told me they weren't willing to accept them. I told them I still wanted to go but a lot happened after that, with the club getting a new manager and being taken over by new owners.

"To be honest, I still wanted to leave. I was thinking, is it going to change anything? Is it going to be a short-term thing which lifts the club for six months and then goes back to how things were before? I spoke to Martin O'Neill and told him I still felt I needed a change, but he dealt with it the right way. He didn't read too much into it, he just got his point across.

"He told me it would be good for him if I stayed until Christmas and then decided how things were going and if I was enjoying it. But over the next couple of weeks I could see that things were changing and the club was going in the right direction. The more I trained with John Robertson and Steve Walford, the more I enjoyed it, and I liked the way the manager was working.

"By the start of the season I was ready to commit to a long-term contract. My mind was on the next four years rather than next Christmas."

GARETH BARRY - CAREER STATS	
BORN:	Hastings
DATE OF BIRTH:	February 23 1981
JOINED VILLA:	July 1997
VILLA LEAGUE APPS:	290
GOALS:	27
VILLA CUP APPS:	62
GOALS	8
INT. CAPS (England):	9
GOALS:	0

ASTON VILLA IN THE PREMIER LEAGUE
BISHOP'S 10 BEST GAMES

While I received considerable assistance in formulating Villa's Perfect 10 Premier League players, this selection of matches is my own choice. For the purpose of consistency, I have avoided cup ties, so the 1994 League Cup home semi-final against Tranmere and the final against Manchester United, plus the UEFA Cup home leg against Inter Milan the same year are not featured. Anyway, here goes, in chronological order:

VILLA 4 LIVERPOOL 2 (19/09/92)

No games were quite as stirring as this one in the inaugural Premier League campaign, on the day Dean Saunders made his Villa home debut against the club he had just left.

After a truly shocking miss by Ronny Rosenthal, who took the ball past Nigel Spink and then hit the bar, former Villa man Mark Walters put the Merseysiders ahead on 43 before Saunders equalised following a superb Steve Froggatt cross.

Rosenthal eventually hit the target six minutes from time, but by then Dalian Atkinson, Saunders and Garry Parker had sent the Holte End into raptures.

VILLA 2 LIVERPOOL 1 (07/05/94)

It was Saunders' "understudy" who took centre stage on the final day of 1993-94. Dwight Yorke was still in the process of establishing himself but he wrote himself into Villa history by scoring twice at the Holte End in the last match before the famous terrace was demolished to make way for an all-seater stand. Robbie Fowler gave Liverpool a 17th-minute lead but sub Yorke struck on 65 and 81 to make it a magnificent finale.

ASTON VILLA IN THE PREMIER LEAGUE
TOTTENHAM HOTSPUR 3 VILLA 4 (19/11/94)

Ron Atkinson had just been sacked, while Gerry Francis was in charge of Tottenham for the first time. But this was the day Villa's caretaker-boss Jim Barron became the Villa manager with a 100 per cent record – one match, one win. And what a win!

It looked like a White Hart Lane whitewash when Villa led 3-0, thanks to two goals from Graham Fenton and one from Dalian Atkinson but then it all started to go wrong.

Without a win in nine matches, Villa were pegged back to 3-3 by the 71st minute and the only likely outcome at that stage was yet another defeat. But right at the end, Dean Saunders lashed home a superb goal to provide a fitting finale to a great piece of entertainment.

VILLA 3 ARSENAL 2 (13/12/98)

One-nil to the Arsenal was usually enough to signal defeat for the Gunners' opponents but on this occasion, even a 2-0 deficit failed to prevent Villa from recording an incredible victory which took them back to the top of the Premiership table.

Dennis Bergkamp fired home an angled shot from the edge of the penalty to give Arsenal a 14th-minute lead before netting the Gunners' second in first-half stoppage time.

But just past the hour mark, the big comeback was underway, Julian Joachim stroking the ball home with the outside of his boot.

Three minutes later, the home side were level, Dion Dublin stabbing in from close range – and seven minutes from the end, it was that man Dublin again, the striker blasting the ball into the roof of the net from close range.

ASTON VILLA IN THE PREMIER LEAGUE
TOTTENHAM HOTSPUR 2 VILLA 4 (15/04/00)

Having almost wasted a three-goal lead at White Hart Lane six years earlier, Villa displayed their battling qualities on this occasion.

They trailed 2-0 just after half-time, to goals from Steffen Iversen and Chris Armstrong and with the FA Cup final only a few weeks away, there was no reason to suppose they would bust a gut to get back in the game. How wrong we were!

Dion Dublin reduced the deficit with a penalty just past the hour mark, and then equalised with a spectacular overhead kick. A minute later Benito Carbone put Villa ahead with a 25-yard volley and Alan Wright did likewise to put the issue beyond doubt. John Gregory's men had scored four in 12 minutes – three of them contenders for Goal of the Season!

VILLA 3 COVENTRY CITY 2 (05/05/01)

The final home match of the 2000-01 season didn't mean a great deal to Villa – at least, not until Coventry City stormed into a two-goal interval lead! Moroccan Moustapha Hadji – later to join Villa – was on target both times and his goals appeared to have thrown the Sky Blues a lifeline in their battle for Premiership survival.

But John Gregory's men had other ideas. Darius Vassell pulled a goal back after an hour, and Villa Park erupted when Juan Pablo Angel, who had endured a torrid time since his £9.5m signing from River Plate, equalised with his first goal for the club. Paul Merson's winner six minutes from the end condemned Coventry to relegation, but it was a day of celebration for the boys in claret and blue.

Perfect 10 matches – Paul Merson celebrates the winner against Coventry (above), while Patrik Berger shows his delight after his Goal of the Season against Sheffield Utd

ASTON VILLA IN THE PREMIER LEAGUE

MIDDLESBROUGH 2 VILLA 5 (28/01/03)

Villa managed just one away success throughout a disappointing 2002-03 campaign – but what a win! They headed to Teesside with apparently little hope of three points against a side who were previously unbeaten at The Riverside, and really turned on the style.

It looked like a false dawn when Darius Vassell and Icelandic debut-boy Joey Gudjonsson established a two-goal advantage after barely half-an-hour. Boro retaliated with two in three minutes from Massimo Maccarone and Jonathan Greening to be level by half-time.

But Gareth Barry restored Villa's lead within two minutes of the resumption, Vassell grabbed his second of the game and Dion Dublin completed a remarkable victory for the claret and blues right at the death.

VILLA 3 CHELSEA 2 (12/04/04)

As Easter treats go, this one takes some beating. Maybe Chelsea weren't quite the phenomenal force they would become over the next couple of years, but it was still a magnificent victory over a team who lay second in the table and had previously lost just five times in 32 league matches.

The Londoners seemed to be on course for another win when they dominated early on and Hernan Crespo gave them an 11th-minute lead. But by the time Crespo scored his second right at the end, Villa had taken control with goals from Darius Vassell, Thomas Hitzlsperger and Lee Hendrie.

ASTON VILLA IN THE PREMIER LEAGUE

VILLA 3 BIRMINGHAM CITY 1 (16/04/06)

The return of the Second City derby had proved to be something of a curse for Villa during Blues' first three seasons in the top flight and all we had to show from six meetings was two draws and four defeats.

But Kevin Phillips stopped the rot with the winner at St. Andrew's in October – and the return match was another one to savour for the claret and blue faithful.

In front of a 40,000-plus crowd, Milan Baros opened the scoring on 10 minutes but the visitors, battling against relegation, were level through Chris Sutton by the interval.

Then came the moment which will live long in Villa memories as young defender Gary Cahill launched himself into the air to beat goalkeeper Maik Taylor with an acrobatic scissors kick. A second Baros goal put the icing on a very tasty cake!

VILLA 3 SHEFFIELD UNITED 0 (05/05/07)

Maybe this was too one-sided to be considered a classic game, but the atmosphere was unbelievable. It was the day Villa supporters saluted members of the 1982 European Cup-winning squad, who paraded on the pitch before the match and then savoured a very special performance from Martin O'Neill's men.

Villa dominated from the outset against the Yorkshire outfit, establishing a two-goal interval lead with well-taken goals from Gabriel Agbonlahor and Ashley Young before Patrik Berger put the seal on a superb performance with Villa's Goal of the Season. Oh, what a perfect day!

ASTON VILLA IN THE PREMIER LEAGUE

LEADING LIGHTS
(As at the end of 2006-07)

Most appearances: Gareth Barry (290)

Most goals: Dwight Yorke (60)

Most goals as sub: Julian Joachim (10)

First goal: Dalian Atkinson

Fastest goal: Dwight Yorke (13 seconds)

Captains:
Kevin Richardson
Shaun Teale
Dean Saunders
Andy Townsend
Gareth Southgate
Ugo Ehiogu
Paul Merson
Peter Schmeichel
Steve Staunton
Olof Mellberg
Gavin McCann
Gareth Barry

Record signing: Juan Pablo Angel (£9.5m)

ASTON VILLA IN THE PREMIER LEAGUE

LEADING LIGHTS
(As at the end of 2006-07)

Hat-trick heroes:

Dean Saunders
Tommy Johnson
Savo Milosevic
Dwight Yorke
Dion Dublin
Luke Moore

Top 10 scorers:

Dwight Yorke (60)
Dion Dublin (48)
Juan Pablo Angel (44)
Dean Saunders (37)
Julian Joachim (32)
Savo Milosevic (28)
Ian Taylor (28)
Lee Hendrie (27)
Gareth Barry (27)
Dalian Atkinson (22)

ASTON VILLA IN THE PREMIER LEAGUE

Top 10 biggest league wins:

7-1	Wimbledon	(h)	11th February, 1995
5-0	Swindon Town	(h)	12th February, 1994
=	Wimbledon	(h)	22nd December, 1996
=	Leicester City	(a)	30th January, 2004
5-1	Middlesbrough	(h)	17th January, 1993
4-0	Watford	(h)	5th February, 2000
=	Middlesbrough	(a)	14th February, 2000
=	Wolves	(a)	14th March, 2004
=	Everton	(h)	26th December, 2005
=	Middlesbrough	(a)	4th February, 2006

Biggest signings:

£9.5m	Juan Pablo Angel (from River Plate, 2001)
£8m	Ashley Young (from Watford, 2007)
£7m	Stan Collymore (from Liverpool, 1997)
=	Milan Baros (from Liverpool, 2005)
=	John Carew (from Lyon, 2007)
£6.75m	Paul Merson (from Middlesbrough, 1998)
£6.5m	Stiliyan Petrov (from Celtic, 2006)
£5.8m	Bosko Balaban (from Dinamo Zagreb, 2001)
£5.75m	Dion Dublin (from Coventry City, 1998)
£5.6m	Alpay Ozalan (from Fenerbahce, 2000)
=	Olof Mellberg (from R. Santander, 2001)
£5.5m	Steve Stone (from Nottingham Forest, 1999)

ASTON VILLA IN THE PREMIER LEAGUE

Highest attendances at Villa Park:

45,374	Liverpool	7th May, 1994
42,632	Man Utd	26th August, 2001
42,602	Birmingham C.	3rd March, 2003
	Man Utd	15th March, 2003
	Arsenal	5th April, 2003
42,593	Liverpool	4th December, 2004
	Man Utd	28th December, 2004
	Arsenal	5th February, 2005
42,573	Liverpool	24th August, 2003
	Tottenham H.	2nd May, 2004
	Man Utd	15th May, 2004
42,551	Liverpool	5th November, 2005
	Tottenham H.	14th October, 2006
	Man Utd	23rd December, 2006
	Liverpool	18th March, 2007
	Sheffield Utd	5th May, 2007

Honours during the Premier League years:

League Cup winners:	1994, 1996
FA Cup finalists:	2000
Intertoto Cup winners:	2001

ASTON VILLA IN THE PREMIER LEAGUE

Top 10 appearances
(substitute appearances in brackets):

Gareth Barry	278 (12 sub)
Alan Wright	255 (5)
Steve Staunton	233 (11)
Ugo Ehiogu	219 (8)
Lee Hendrie	202 (48)
Ian Taylor	202 (31)
Olof Mellberg	198
Gareth Southgate	191
Mark Bosnich	178
Dwight Yorke	160 (19)

The men in charge:

Ron Atkinson	(June 1991-November 1994)
Brian Little	(November 1994-February 1998)
John Gregory	(February 1998-January 2002)
Graham Taylor	(February 2002-May 2003)
David O'Leary	(May 2003-July 2006)
Martin O'Neill	(August 2006-)

ASTON VILLA IN THE PREMIER LEAGUE

Season-by-season record:

Season	Pos	P	W	D	L	F	A	Pts
92-93	2nd	42	21	11	10	57	40	74
93-94	10th	42	15	12	15	46	50	57
94-95	18th	42	11	15	16	51	56	48
95-96	4th	38	18	· 9	11	52	35	63
96-97	5th	38	17	10	11	47	34	61
97-98	7th	38	17	6	15	49	48	57
98-99	6th	38	15	10	13	51	46	55
99-00	6th	38	15	13	10	46	35	58
00-01	8th	38	13	15	10	46	43	54
01-02	8th	38	12	14	12	46	47	50
02-03	16th	38	12	9	17	42	47	45
03-04	6th	38	15	11	12	48	44	56
04-05	10th	38	12	11	15	45	52	47
05-06	16th	38	10	12	16	42	55	42
06-07	11th	38	11	17	10	43	41	50

ASTON VILLA IN THE PREMIER LEAGUE

THE CAST
(In order of appearance)

1992-93

Nigel Spink, Earl Barrett, Steve Staunton,
Shaun Teale, Paul McGrath, Kevin Richardson,
Tony Daley, Garry Parker, Ray Houghton,
Dalian Atkinson, Steve Froggatt, Cyrille Regis,
Dwight Yorke, Frank McAvennie, Ugo Ehiogu,
Dean Saunders, Mark Blake, Bryan Small,
Dave Farrell, Neil Cox, Mark Bosnich,
Matthias Breitkreutz, Stefan Beinlich,
Martin Carruthers.

1993-94

Andy Townsend, Gordon Cowans, Guy Whittingham,
Dariusz Kubicki, Graham Fenton.

1994-95

John Fashanu, Phil King, Nii Lamptey, Chris Boden,
Ian Taylor, Tommy Johnson, Gary Charles,
Franz Carr, Alan Wright.

ASTON VILLA IN THE PREMIER LEAGUE

THE CAST
(In order of appearance)

1995-96

Gareth Southgate, Mark Draper, Savo Milosevic,
Riccardo Scimeca, Carl Tiler, Lee Hendrie,
Gareth Farrelly, Julian Joachim, Paul Browne,
Scott Murray, Neil Davis.

1996-97

Michael Oakes, Sasa Curcic, Fernando Nelson,
David Hughes.

1997-98

Stan Collymore, Simon Grayson, Darren Byfield,
Richard Walker, Gareth Barry.

1998-99

Alan Thompson, Darius Vassell, Paul Merson,
Steve Watson, Dion Dublin, Adam Rachel,
Steve Stone, Colin Calderwood, Mark Delaney.

ASTON VILLA IN THE PREMIER LEAGUE

THE CAST
(In order of appearance)

1999-00

David James, George Boateng, Peter Enckelman,
Benito Carbone, Najwan Ghrayib, Jlloyd Samuel,
Neil Cutler, Jonathan Bewers.

2000-01

Alpay Ozalan, David Ginola, Luc Nilis,
Gilles De Bilde, John McGrath, Thomas Hitzlsperger,
Juan Pablo Angel.

2001-02

Peter Schmeichel, Olof Mellberg, Hassan Kachloul,
Moustapha Hadji, Bosko Balaban, Peter Crouch.

2002-03

Ulises De la Cruz, Marcus Allback, Mark Kinsella,
Ronny Johnsen, Stefan Moore, Stefan Postma,
Oyvind Leonhardsen, Rob Edwards,
Stephen Cooke, Joey Gudjonsson,
Peter Whittingham.

ASTON VILLA IN THE PREMIER LEAGUE

THE CAST
(In order of appearance)

2003-04

Thomas Sorensen, Gavin McCann, Liam Ridgewell,
Nobby Solano, Luke Moore.

2004-05

Martin Laursen, Carlton Cole, Steven Davis, Mathieu Berson,
Eric Djemba-Djemba.

2005-06

Aaron Hughes, Kevin Phillips, Milan Baros,
Patrik Berger, Wilfred Bouma, James Milner,
Eirik Bakke, Stuart Taylor, Craig Gardner,
Gabriel Agbonlahor, Gary Cahill.

2006-07

Stiliyan Petrov, Didier Agathe, Chris Sutton,
Isaiah Osbourne, Gabor Kiraly, Phil Bardsley,
Ashley Young, John Carew, Shaun Maloney.

ALSO AVAILABLE IN THE SERIES